HIGH TIME TO AWAKE

CRAIG C. WHITE

NATION BY NATION

VERSE BY VERSE

Syria, Turkey, Sudan, Egypt, Russia,
United States, Jordan, Iran, Kurds

CRAIG C. WHITE

Copyright 2013 Craig C. White

HIGH TIME TO AWAKE

NATION BY NATION

VERSE BY VERSE

Available from Amazon.com, CreateSpace.com, and other retail outlets. Also available on Kindle and other devices.

Some photos used under creative commons attribution 2.0 Generic (CC BY 2.0) creativecommons.org

Cover and interior flags courtesy of The World Factbook at www.cia.gov
Bible references are from the King James Version.

First edition published by High Time to Awake 2014

www.hightimetoawake.com

Jesus: Thank you for your forgiveness and for the illumination to understand the things that are written in your book so that I might be able to write this book.

Yours, Craig C. White

Just before Israel's seven year period of Tribulation the nations in the old world will fight against one another.

Luke 21:10 Then said he unto them, Nation shall rise against nation, and kingdom against kingdom:

There are a lot of nations mentioned in the bible. Did you know that the bible usually identifies each nation by name?! Sometimes the bible identifies an ancient nation by the name of its provinces or cities. In most instances these ancient names are still being used today! So identifying modern day nations that are listed in the bible is not too difficult.

The bible records the history of these nations especially when their history also affects the nation of Israel. The bible also predicts the future actions of these nations.

In the bible the *nations* are also called *gentiles* or *heathen*. The gentile nations are simply the original families that settled their own countries after Noah's flood. These are the same nations in the Middle East, Northern Egypt, and Central Asia that we still know today. Most of these nations have rebelled against the God of Israel since their beginnings. End time bible prophecy centers upon the trouble that Israel will endure under the rule of the next World Empire. All of these nations will oppress the nation of Israel during their time of tribulation.

This book identifies a few key nations who will play significant roles during the years leading up to and during Israel's time of trouble. We will take a verse by verse look at specific prophetic events that these nations will fulfill. I expect that these prophecies reflect the near time future of world history.

Contents

NATION BY NATION
VERSE BY VERSE

Who is Fighting in Syria?

Bible verses about Eagles Wings

www.hightimetoawake.com

More from High Time to Awake

Available from Amazon.com, CreateSpace.com, and other retail outlets. Also available on Kindle and other devices.

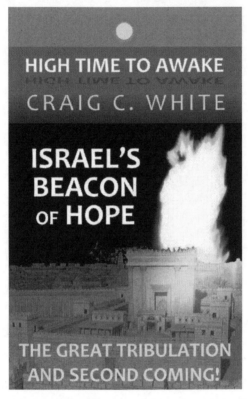

Israel's Beacon of Hope chronicles the trial of the nation of Israel during the Great Tribulation period. Happily it also explores the return of the Shekinah glory to Jerusalem, the return of all believing Jews throughout time to Israel, and life after the Tribulation. God's covenant with Israel is everlasting!

www.hightimetoawake.com

Preface

Why do the Nations Rage?

Palmerworm, locust, cankerworm, and caterpillar.

Psalm 2, Acts 4

By Craig C. White

Note: The sign reads, "Down with Omar Suleiman, Israel man". Omar Suleiman is Egypt's top intelligence chief. He was appointed vice-president by Hosni Mubarak on January 29, 2011. Suleiman has an anti-Islamism view and is sympathetic toward Israel. Photo credit: Monasosh

Throughout the Middle East and northern Africa the nations are exercising their "Days of Rage". It has been widely proclaimed by the media that the nations are fighting to establish democracy. While some hope for

9

democracy; *Rage* is induced by a different impulse. King David illuminates this timely question. "Why do the heathen rage, and the people imagine a vain thing?"

Psa 2:1-12 Why do the heathen rage, and the people imagine a vain thing? 2 The kings of the earth set themselves, and the rulers take counsel together, against the LORD, and against his anointed, saying, 3 Let us break their bands asunder, and cast away their cords from us. 4 He that sitteth in the heavens shall laugh: the Lord shall have them in derision. 5 Then shall he speak unto them in his wrath, and vex them in his sore displeasure. 6 Yet have I set my king upon my holy hill of Zion. 7 I will declare the decree: the LORD hath said unto me, Thou art my Son; this day have I begotten thee. 8 Ask of me, and I shall give thee the heathen for thine inheritance, and the uttermost parts of the earth for thy possession. 9 Thou shalt break them with a rod of iron; thou shalt dash them in pieces like a potter's vessel. 10 Be wise now therefore, O ye kings: be instructed, ye judges of the earth. 11 Serve the LORD with fear, and rejoice with trembling. 12 Kiss the Son, lest he be angry, and ye perish from the way, when his wrath is kindled but a little. Blessed are all they that put their trust in him.

Why do the Heathen Rage? Let's take this one verse at a time.

Psa 2:2 The kings of the earth set themselves, and the rulers take counsel together, against the LORD, and against his anointed, saying,

The LORD's anointed is Jesus Christ. The baptism of Jesus and his anointing with the Holy Spirit is recorded in all four gospels. This anointing of the Holy Spirit and the witness of God's own voice prove that Jesus is the Son of God. We also have the following report of an eye-witness, namely John the Baptist. In the mouth of two or three witnesses shall every word be established.

Mar 1:9-11 And it came to pass in those days, that Jesus came from Nazareth of Galilee, and was baptized of John in Jordan. 10 And straightway coming up out of the water, he saw the heavens opened, and the Spirit like a dove descending upon him: 11 And there came a voice from heaven, saying, Thou art my beloved Son, in whom I am well pleased.

Psa 2:3-5 Let us break their bands asunder, and cast away their cords from us. 4 He that sitteth in the heavens shall laugh: the Lord shall have them in derision. 5 Then shall he speak unto them in his wrath, and vex them in his sore displeasure.

Why do the Heathen Rage? Here is the answer to our question. The heathen declare they will remove any authority or accountability that God the father or his Son have over them. This is of course impossible. God laughs at their opposition. Created earthly powers cannot compare with his power. They are too far inferior. God is above everything and separate from his creation.

Rebellion is a certain type of sin. It is more insidious than sexual immorality or murder or theft. Rebellion is refusing to humble oneself under the authority of the one true God. The result of rebellion is everlasting punishment.

Joh 3:36 He that believeth on the Son hath everlasting life: and he that believeth not the Son shall not see life; but the wrath of God abideth on him.

The nations rage in order to break accountability to God. This vain rage results in Israel's sore distress. In "the day of the Lord", God will break the yoke that the heathen has placed on the neck of Israel. Israel will no longer have to bend to international pressure to give up their land or defend their right to exist.

Jer 30:8 For it shall come to pass in that day, saith the LORD of hosts, that I will break his yoke from off thy neck, and will burst thy bonds, and strangers shall no more serve themselves of him:

Psa 2:6-9 Yet have I set my king upon my holy hill of Zion. 7 I will declare the decree: the LORD hath said unto me, Thou art my Son; this day have I begotten thee. 8 Ask of me, and I shall give thee the heathen for thine inheritance, and the uttermost parts of the earth for thy possession. 9 Thou shalt break them with a rod of iron; thou shalt dash them in pieces like a potter's vessel.

After the "heathen rage" God places Jesus upon his everlasting throne in Jerusalem and gives him great honor. All nations are put under the authority of Jesus Christ. They are his to rule and judge forever.

Psa 2:10-12 Be wise now therefore, O ye kings: be instructed, ye judges of the earth. 11 Serve the LORD with fear, and rejoice with trembling. 12 Kiss the Son, lest he be angry, and ye perish from the way, when his wrath is kindled but a little. Blessed are all they that put their trust in him.

Kings, Presidents, Governors listen up! When Jesus is king on earth; he will reign with an iron rod. He will not tolerate dissent. My advice is that you begin serving him now.

Who are the heathen? They are the nations of people who settled the world after Noah's flood. What does the original Hebrew term go'ee or goyim mean? "Goyim" is commonly translated as nations, heathen, or gentiles in the English bible. According to "Strong's Hebrew and Greek Dictionaries" the root of go'ee refers to a massing of people, nations, animals, or locusts etc.

go'ee (in the sense of massing); a foreign nation; hence a Gentile; also (figuratively) a troop of animals, or a flight of locusts: - Gentile, heathen, nation, people.

In Joel's three short chapters, God warns Israel that a nation is coming against them who are like locusts. **There are a lot of them and they leave a path of destruction.** Babylon partly fulfilled this prophecy in 608-585 B.C. Babylon attacked Judah on three different occasions. Joel's prophecy also refers to a future invasion just prior to the great and the terrible day of the Lord (Joel 1:15, 2:1, 2:31, and 3:14). Palmerworm, locust, cankerworm, and caterpillar are all referring to types of locusts.

Joe 1:4 That which the palmerworm hath left hath the locust eaten; and that which the locust hath left hath the cankerworm eaten; and that which the cankerworm hath left hath the caterpiller eaten. 5 Awake, ye drunkards, and weep; and howl, all ye drinkers of wine, because of the new wine; for it is cut off from your mouth. 6 For a nation is come up upon my land, strong, and without number, whose teeth are the teeth of a lion, and he hath the cheek teeth of a great lion.

The locusts look like horses with teeth of a lion!

Joe 2:4-5 The appearance of them is as the appearance of horses; and as horsemen, so shall they run. 5 Like the noise of chariots on the tops of mountains shall they leap, like the noise of a flame of fire that devoureth the stubble, as a strong people set in battle array.

The description of the locusts in revelation is nearly identical to that in Joel.

Rev 9:7-11 And the shapes of the locusts were like unto horses prepared unto battle; and on their heads were as it were crowns like gold, and their faces were as the faces of men. 8 And they had hair as the hair of women, and their teeth were as the teeth of lions. 9 And they had breastplates, as it were breastplates of iron; and the sound of their wings was as the sound of chariots of many horses running to battle. 10 And they had tails like unto scorpions, and there were stings in their tails: and their power was to hurt men five months. 11 And they had a king over them, which is the angel of the bottomless pit, whose name in the Hebrew tongue is Abaddon, but in the Greek tongue hath his name Apollyon.

So, according to the root definition of the Hebrew word "goyim" and the prophet Joel, the heathen will invade Israel like locusts.

Why do the heathen rage, and the people imagine a vain thing? After the death and resurrection of Jesus the apostles Peter and John remember King David's question.

Act 4:25-28 Who by the mouth of thy servant David hast said, Why did the heathen rage, and the people imagine vain things? 26 The kings of the earth stood up, and the rulers were gathered together against the Lord, and against his Christ. 27 For of a truth against thy holy child Jesus, whom thou hast anointed, both Herod, and Pontius Pilate, with the Gentiles, and the people of Israel, were gathered together, 28 For to do whatsoever thy hand and thy counsel determined before to be done.

In Acts 4 the heathen rage and put Jesus to death. Perhaps heathen today reason they can accomplish this again. They forget that Jesus Christ rose from the dead. God raised him up, because it was not possible that death could hold him (Acts 2:24).

Act 2:24 Whom God hath raised up, having loosed the pains of death: because it was not possible that he should be holden of it.

Christ's death does not satisfy King David's prophecy. The heathen are raging again. This time God will place Jesus upon his everlasting throne in Jerusalem.

Psa 2:6-9 Yet have I set my king upon my holy hill of Zion. 7 I will declare the decree: the LORD hath said unto me, Thou art my Son; this day have I begotten thee. 8 Ask of me, and I shall give thee the heathen for

14

thine inheritance, and the uttermost parts of the earth for thy possession. 9 Thou shalt break them with a rod of iron; thou shalt dash them in pieces like a potter's vessel.

God asked the question, why do the heathen rage? Today the world is answering that question. Of course they are giving the wrong answer. God knew they would. He gave the question as a sign of the end times. The heathen are raging and we are very close to Christ's coming for his Church and the Great Tribulation.

SECTION 1: SYRIA

The city of Damascus is the capital of Syria. It is a large prosperous city with modern amenities and an ancient history. Damascus is one of the oldest inhabited cities in the world. It was founded by the Aramaeans over four thousand years ago, and was inhabited two thousand years before that. Damascus is a living depiction of human history. Today Damascus is dying.

According to Old Testament prophets Isaiah and Jeremiah; Damascus, Syria will be destroyed. Syria has been fighting for its sovereignty for the past three years. I think that the bible tells us that Turkey will eventually enter Syria and destroy Damascus. This could be the prophetic event that puts the end time into high gear!

Chapter One

Damascus Syria in Bible Prophecy

Syrian opposition flag photo credit: Freedom House
http://www.flickr.com/

The destruction of Damascus may be a prelude to the battle of Gog and Magog!

By Craig C. White

The destruction of Damascus Syria is the next event to look for on the prophetic calendar. The city of Damascus, Syria may soon be destroyed as Isaiah 17:1 and Jeremiah 49:24-27 predicts.

Damascus is the capital of Syria and its second largest city, with about 2.6 million people in the metropolitan area. Today Syria is in the midst of a battle for its sovereignty. There is a movement to oust Syrian President Bashar Assad. While most Syrians support the more westernized Assad, Islamist factions led by the Muslim Brotherhood are fighting for control of the country. Today foreign jihadists are fighting the Syrian army near the city of Damascus. Damascus has already suffered some damage, but according to Isaiah 17: 1 Damascus will be *taken away from being a city*. Today, fighting in Damascus is on the rise.

World governments are scrambling. The UN and US leadership want Syrian President Assad gone. The CIA has been smuggling weapons to the Muslim Brotherhood in Syria as well as providing flour and funding. Russia and Iran want Assad to stay. The US is pushing for Middle Eastern led military action. The US, UN, Britain, France, Saudi Arabia, Turkey, and other world powers are pushing for an escalation of force to oust the Syrian President. In July 2015 NATO gave its approval for the Turkish Army to enter Syria.

Up until now Turkey had hoped that the Rebels would eventually overtake the Syrian army. The key to victory is to capture of the seat of power in Damascus. However, rebel fighters say that they do not have the military might to take Damascus. In July 2015 Turkey deployed 54,000 troops and heavy artillery along the Syrian border. NATO has deployed several Patriot missile batteries as well. The missiles are manned by 400 US soldiers. It looks like foreign military force will be brought to bear soon.

In Isaiah 17 the city of Damascus is prophesied to be destroyed. Damascus was conquered once already when Assyria invaded Syria and northern Israel in 734 B.C. However, the bible predicts its complete destruction. Bible prophecy often represents two similar events usually separated by time. Conditions are ripe for a present day destruction of Damascus.

Isa 17:1 The burden of Damascus. Behold, Damascus is taken away from being a city, and it shall be a ruinous heap.

Jeremiah chapter 49 below suggests that Damascus (metro population 2.6 million) will turn to flee. Today many Syrians have already fled the fighting; seeking refuge in

Turkey, Jordan, Lebanon and other regional countries. There are currently almost 4,000,000 Syrian refugees in surrounding countries. Over nine million Syrians have left their homes. Many Syrians have taken refuge in Damascus. Hundreds of thousands of Syrians have also fled from Damascus as the fighting drew nearer. Attention: High Alert! Bible prophecy is unfolding concerning Damascus.

Jer 49:24-27 Damascus is waxed feeble, and turneth herself to flee, and fear hath seized on her: anguish and sorrows have taken her, as a woman in travail. 25 How is the city of praise not left, the city of my joy! 26 Therefore her young men shall fall in her streets, and all the men of war shall be cut off in that day, saith the LORD of hosts. 27 And I will kindle a fire in the wall of Damascus, and it shall consume the palaces of Benhadad.

Note: Benhadad is the title of several Syrian kings who ruled in Damascus (1 Kings 15:18).

In Jeremiah 49:27 (above) God will *kindle a fire in the wall of Damascus*. To "kindle a fire" means that God will send an army to invade Damascus. Turkish troops are lined up along the Syrian border. Tensions are heating up between the Syrian and Turkish armies. I think that God may be sending the Turkish army against Damascus.

The Prophet Amos also condemns Damascus. This prophecy was fulfilled when Tiglath-pileser the Assyrian king conquered Damascus in 734 B.C. and carried the Syrian (Aramean) captives away to Kir a mountainous region in western Jordan. However, like many bible prophecies this may also refer to a current event. Today the region of Kir in Jordan is called Kerak. There are about one half million Syrian refugees in Kerak today. This is further evidence that the destruction of Damascus as described in the bible is imminent. It is also evidence that the God of Israel is the one true God and that we all had better heed his word and we had also better humble ourselves before him

19

while there is still time! In verse 5 the plain of Aven is a valley in the northeast part of Lebanon near the Syrian border. Today it is called the Bekaa valley. It has been suggested that Saddam Hussein hid WMD's here before the US invasion of Iraq.

Amos 1:3-5 Thus saith the LORD; For three transgressions of Damascus, and for four, I will not turn away the punishment thereof; because they have threshed Gilead with threshing instruments of iron: 4 But I will send a fire into the house of Hazael, which shall devour the palaces of Benhadad. 5 I will break also the bar of Damascus, and cut off the inhabitant from the plain of Aven, and him that holdeth the sceptre from the house of Eden: and the people of Syria shall go into captivity unto Kir, saith the LORD.

Talk of a military conflict between Israel and Iran is also on the rise. In Ezekiel chapter 38 a Turkish led invasion into Israel is described. Turkey is Joined by Iran, Ethiopia/Sudan (The original Hebrew word Cush more accurately describes Sudan), and Libya. It may be that shortly after the destruction of Damascus a Middle East invasion into Israel will occur.

In Ezekiel 38:4 below God is talking to the leader of Turkey.

Eze 38:4-5 And I will turn thee back, and put hooks into thy jaws, and I will bring thee forth, and all thine army, horses and horsemen, all of them clothed with all sorts of armour, even a great company with bucklers and shields, all of them handling swords: 5 Persia, Ethiopia, and Libya with them; all of them with shield and helmet:

I am convinced that Turkish President Recep Tayyip Erdogan is the modern day fulfillment of Magog the primary leader of the land of Turkey described in Ezekiel chapter 38. So I expect the battle of Gog and Magog to

20

happen soon! Turkey may destroy Damascus. Turkey may also then lead a Middle Eastern invasion into Israel. It is High Time to Awake and watch!

More from High Time to Awake

Available from Amazon.com, CreateSpace.com, and other retail outlets. Also available on Kindle and other devices.

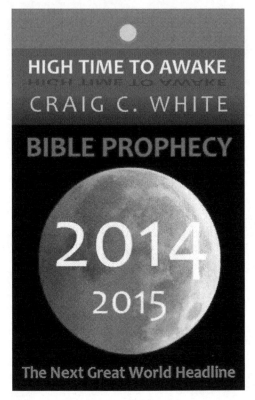

Bible Prophecy 2014-2015: Welcome to 2014. Bible prophecy is unfolding everywhere. The heathen are raging in the Middle East. Egyptian is fighting Egyptian. Christians are being killed and tormented more than ever. The New World Order is old news. An international security agreement and Palestinian state are being forged for the nation of Israel. All of these events have been foretold in bible prophecy. **Bible Prophecy 2014-2015** tells us what to expect in the coming two years.

www.hightimetoawake.com

Chapter Two

Isaiah 17 predicts the destruction of Damascus

Umayyad Mosque, Damascus photo credit: Jan Smith
http://www.flickr.com/

Photo info: The Umayyad Mosque, or the Grand Mosque of Damascus, is one of the largest and oldest mosques in the world, completed in 715 AD.

Ruin, Respect, Rush, Rebuke

A verse by verse study through Isaiah chapter 17

By Craig C. White

Isaiah chapter 17 predicts the destruction of Damascus. There is a rule in bible prophecy that some predictions apply to two separate events usually separated by a long span of time. I guess you could say that God instructs us to learn about future events by observing past events. Much of the prophecy in Isaiah 17 was fulfilled during the Assyrian invasion of Damascus in 734 BC. However, Damascus was not destroyed at that time. As a matter of fact it continued as an important city of the Assyrian Empire. So Isaiah's dire predictions may also apply to future events.

Damascus is under siege today. A lot of bible buffs say that Damascus will be destroyed suddenly. They say that Damascus will probably be obliterated by a nuclear bomb. I don't see that scenario communicated in scripture. Instead Jeremiah 49:27 says, "I will kindle a fire in the wall of Damascus". This terminology is used several times in the Old Testament. To *kindle a fire* means that God will send an invading army against Damascus; just as God sent the Assyrian army to invade Damascus in 734 BC.

God has certainly sent an army against Damascus today. The "Free Syrian Army" is fighting in Damascus against the Syrian Army. The Free Syrian Army consists mostly of Libyan Al-Qaeda fighters. By the way, after Assyria invaded Damascus they turned south into Israel. It is possible that the armies invading Damascus today may also turn south to come against Israel. We are allowed to learn from past events!

Isa 17:1-2 The burden of Damascus. Behold, Damascus is taken away from *being* a city, and it shall be a ruinous heap. 2 The cities of Aroer *are* forsaken: they shall be for flocks, which shall lie down, and none shall make *them* afraid.

There are several Middle Eastern cities called Aroer, but this Aroer most probably refers to the southern region of Syria. The cities of Aroer refer to Damascus and its nearby cities. The destruction described here may even spill over into nearby Lebanon.

Remember that these verses most directly apply to the past Assyrian invasion of Damascus. After Assyria conquered Syria they then invaded northern Israel and carried away captives. In verse 3 below *Ephraim* refers to the northern kingdom of Israel. God is saying that Syria as well as northern Israel will be conquered and carried away captive so that not many people are left in their land. This is exactly what happened long ago. Assyria took Syrians captive into north western Jordan and Israel was carried away into today's northern Iraq! The following verses definitely describe what happened long ago, but they also seem to describe a future destruction of Syria and northern Israel. During Israel's future seven year "Tribulation" period only a few Jews will remain in the entire land of Israel (Zechariah 13-14). Perhaps Isaiah is telling us that Israel's Time of trouble follows closely after the future Destruction of Damascus.

Isa 17:3-6 The fortress also shall cease from Ephraim, and the kingdom from Damascus, and the remnant of Syria: they shall be as the glory of the children of Israel, saith the LORD of hosts. 4 And in that day it shall come to pass, *that* **the glory of Jacob shall be made thin, and the fatness of his flesh shall wax lean. 5 And it shall be as when the harvestman gathereth the corn, and reapeth the ears with his arm; and it shall be as he that gathereth ears in the valley of Rephaim. 6 Yet gleaning grapes shall be left in it, as the shaking of an olive tree, two** *or* **three berries in the top of the uppermost bough, four** *or* **five in the outmost fruitful branches thereof, saith the LORD God of Israel.**

Isaiah 17:6 above tells us that a few Jews will be left living in Israel. This is God's way of telling us that a future restoration of the people and land of Israel is possible!

Guess what? Isaiah is finished talking about Damascus. In verse 7 below God is describing the Jewish people's response during a time of national distress. Perhaps this describes Israel's behavior during the Tribulation period. Isaiah is saying that Israel will act respectfully toward God but will still suffer judgment. They will honor God outwardly and not look to false Gods. However, verse 10 explains that the Jews have not truly remembered their

God. These verses may be explaining a period of national recognition of Old Testament laws and practices, such as renewed temple sacrifices during the Tribulation period (Dan 9:27).

Isa 17:7-11 At that day shall a man look to his Maker, and his eyes shall have respect to the Holy One of Israel. 8 And he shall not look to the altars, the work of his hands, neither shall respect *that* which his fingers have made, either the groves, or the images. 9 In that day shall his strong cities be as a forsaken bough, and an uppermost branch, which they left because of the children of Israel: and there shall be desolation. 10 Because thou hast forgotten the God of thy salvation, and hast not been mindful of the rock of thy strength, therefore shalt thou plant pleasant plants, and shalt set it with strange slips: 11 In the day shalt thou make thy plant to grow, and in the morning shalt thou make thy seed to flourish: *but* the harvest *shall be* a heap in the day of grief and of desperate sorrow.

Israel will suffer for their past and present neglect of God. Isaiah explains this in the verse below. Jesus quoted Isaiah in Matthew 15:8.

Isa 29:13 Wherefore the Lord said, Forasmuch as this people draw near *me* with their mouth, and with their lips do honour me, but have removed their heart far from me, and their fear toward me is taught by the precept of men:

Now for something completely different! Isaiah 17:12-14 below describes a multi-nation invasion into Israel. These verses refer to an event that happened around 701 BC. Assyria's king Sennacherib was in position to attack the city of Jerusalem. Overnight, God wiped out his army while they slept. Isaiah describes God's intervention below.

Isa 37:36 Then the angel of the LORD went forth, and smote in the camp of the Assyrians a hundred and fourscore and five thousand: and when they arose early in the morning, behold, they *were* all dead corpses.

The following verses may also describe a future intervention. As a matter of fact I think they may describe two future interventions by God to save Israel!

The terminology of *rushing waters* and *floods* are often used in bible prophecy to describe a large scale overwhelming military invasion.

Isa 17:12-14 Woe to the multitude of many people, *which* make a noise like the noise of the seas; and to the rushing of nations, *that* make a rushing like the rushing of mighty waters! 13 The nations shall rush like the rushing of many waters: but *God* shall rebuke them, and they shall flee far off, and shall be chased as the chaff of the mountains before the wind, and like a rolling thing before the whirlwind. 14 And behold at eveningtide trouble; *and* before the morning he *is* not. This *is* the portion of them that spoil us, and the lot of them that rob us.

Ezekiel chapter 38 describes a multi-national invasion into Israel led by Turkey. God fights against these armies with rain, fire, and confusion. Every nation listed in Ezekiel 38 is currently fighting in Syria. Isaiah may be telling us about a Turkish led invasion into Israel that soon follows the near time destruction of Damascus. Turkey will be joined by the Free Syrian Army made up mostly of Libyan soldiers, and Hezbollah militia from Iran and Sudan.

Isaiah 17:12-14 may also describe the judgment of the nations by Jesus Christ after his second coming at the end of the Tribulation period. However, let me say this. The judgment of the nations by Jesus is described in much more horrid terms, and on a much broader scale elsewhere in the bible. I think that Isaiah 17's rebuke by God may be a more localized event. In other words, it may describe a battle and not the entire war.

Let's remember that these events were all preceded by the destruction of Damascus, Syria. It is high time to awake to the Damascus alarm. Israel will soon suffer its seven year period of indignation. Jesus Christ will soon save Israel from peril. Before all that, Jesus Christ will come in the clouds to resurrect and to gather every Christian who has trusted him since his own resurrection, body and soul!

Chapter Three

The Nations are disquieted over Syria

Jeremiah 49:23-27

By Craig C. White

Jeremiah chapter 49 gives us a blow by blow description of the destruction of Damascus, Syria.

Jeremiah 49:23 Concerning Damascus. Hamath is confounded, and Arpad: for they have heard evil tidings: they are fainthearted; there is sorrow on the sea; it cannot be quiet.

What is Jeremiah telling us? Obviously this prophecy is concerning Damascus, Syria. In the verse above, Jeremiah mentions two cities. Hamath and Arpad are both located in northwestern Syria. Today Hamah is Syria's fourth largest city with a population of 313 thousand. Hamah is further south but still close to the Turkish border. Arpad is modern city of tell Erfad (or Tell Rifaat) about 25 miles north of Aleppo and about 20 miles south of the Turkish border. These cities are along the path of an invasion launched from Turkey headed towards Damascus.

In Jeremiah 49:23 the people of northwestern Syria have heard intelligence reports that the Turkish Army is about to invade Syria. The army's target is Damascus and they are coming through their cities! The people of northwestern Syria are terrified. Their hearts faint with fear

There is sorrow on the sea; it cannot be quiet. The *sea* in bible prophecy can refer to the Mediterranean Sea when it is accompanied with the definite article "the". The *sea* can also refer to the nations of the world. There is no definite article used here in the original Hebrew. So I think that Jeremiah is saying that the nations will have great anxiety over the coming Turkish invasion into Syria. The Hebrew word translated *sorrow* means *anxiety, fearfulness, carefulness,* or *heaviness.*

So the nations will be very nervous concerning the coming Turkish invasion into Syria. The Turkish Army's goal is the destruction of Damascus. The English translation says it well here. The nations will not be able to be still. The Hebrew word translated *quiet* is defined below. The nations of the world will not be able to be at rest. I think that they are already feeling uneasy concerning Syria.

Quiet – shaqat, *shaw-kat'*

A primitive root; to *repose* (usually figuratively): – appease, idleness, (at, be at, be in, give) quiet (-ness), (be at, be in, give, have, take) rest, settle, be still.

Jeremiah 49:24 Damascus is waxed feeble, and turneth herself to flee, and fear hath seized on her: anguish and sorrows have taken her, as a woman in travail.

Damascus is waxed feeble. This is the idea of failing in your old age. Damascus is about to die. Damascus *turneth herself to flee.* This could refer to the city preparing to relinquish its life and it could also refer to the city's inhabitants as they attempt to escape.

The Hebrew word translated *fear* means to *tremble* with *terror. Anguish and sorrows have taken her, as a woman in travail;* literally means that Damascus is feeling a *localized tightness* like a woman about to give birth.

Jeremiah 49:25 How is the city of praise not left, the city of my joy!

Two different Hebrew words for *city* are used in the verse above. *The city of praise* is a fortified city that has been celebrated in song. When God says "how is the city not left" he could be communicating his astonishment that even after a terrible assault on Damascus, the city has not yet surrendered. When God calls Damascus "the city of my joy!'" he is specifically saying that he delights in the city's old buildings. Damascus is the oldest continually inhabited city on earth. It was founded by the Aramaeans over four thousand years ago, and was inhabited two thousand years before that. Damascus is a living depiction of human history.

Jeremiah 49:26 Therefore her young men shall fall in her streets, and all the men of war shall be cut off in that day, saith the LORD of hosts.

In this verse the *young men* are contrasted to *the men of war*. It sounds like the young men of Damascus will stay behind to defend the city. Perhaps they will be the first line of defense. Today, Syria has formed a new civilian National Guard called the "National Defense Force". I think that they may indeed be represented by the *young men* in this verse. The young men of Damascus will die in its streets. The Syrian army will be bunkered in Damascus. When God says that "all the men of war shall be cut off" he means that *all* of the Syrian Army in Damascus will die. When Jeremiah says "in that day" he isn't necessarily saying that this assault on Damascus will last only one day. *That day* refers to the entire duration be it one day or longer.

Jeremiah 49:27 And I will kindle a fire in the wall of Damascus, and it shall consume the palaces of Benhadad.

Let's remember that this prophecy refers to two separate invasions of Damascus. The first invasion happened in 734 BC. The Assyrian Empire invaded Syria, overthrowing several cities as they marched toward Damascus. The Assyrian Army conquered Damascus but did not destroy the city. I think that Jeremiah is also prophesying about a second invasion of Damascus that seems to be forming now. God used the terminology *kindle a fire* to mean that the Assyrian army would besiege the city. Just as the ancient Assyrians assaulted Damascus in 734 BC, I think that the Turkish Army will do likewise. *The palaces of Benhadad* refer to the thrones of ancient Syrian Kings in Damascus. Like the ancient invasion, this future invasion will also destroy Syria's seat of government in Damascus.

So the Turkish army will march down from Syria's northwestern border terrorizing cities along the way. Their goal is the destruction of Damascus. The nations of the world will be in a tumult. They will not be able to calm down. Damascus will prepare to die. The people will flee and the young men and army will fight to the death never surrendering. The oldest city on earth will be destroyed along with its historical buildings. Jeremiah describes a city under siege not a city obliterated by a single bomb.

Chapter Four

Intelligence reports reach Hamath

Turkey prepares to attack Damascus

By Craig C. White

Turkey's parliament just passed a mandate that allows the Turkish army to enter Syria over the next year. Turkish involvement in Syria has been protested by the Turkish people for the past few years. According to Jeremiah 49 Damascus will suffer attack and be destroyed.

Jeremiah 49:23 says that intelligence reports of the attack will come to Syria's northwestern cities. The attack emanates from Turkish border!

Jeremiah 49:23 Concerning Damascus. Hamath is confounded, and Arpad: for they have heard evil tidings: they are fainthearted; there is sorrow on the sea; it cannot be quiet.

Guess what? Syria's northwestern cities are hearing those intelligence reports now!

Starting in early September 2013 Turkey began moving heavy military equipment along Syria's northwestern border. Turkey's military equipment includes tanks, rocket-launchers, missile launchers, and anti-aircraft guns. Turkish military planes have also flown in to the region; those include F-16 fighters, tanker, and cargo planes.

We have been told that Syria may have used chemical weapons, and that justifies overthrowing the Syrian government. Don't be fooled. Whether or not Syria used chemical weapons; world powers will overthrow Syria. Jeremiah 49:25-27 tells us that Damascus will be besieged. The Syrians will not surrender; and all of the young men and Syrian army will be killed inside of the city.

I suspect that intelligence reports of a gathering attack will continue to increase. The next events that Jeremiah records are of terrified citizens in Damascus as they flee the city running for their lives. Damascus has a population of about 2.6 million in the metropolitan area. Hundreds of thousands of Damascus residents have already fled the city. Hundreds of thousands of Syrian refugees have also fled to Damascus from outlying areas. I suspect that the entire city will empty except for the young men and the Syrian Army (Jeremiah 49:26).

Chapter Five

Kir is Kerak

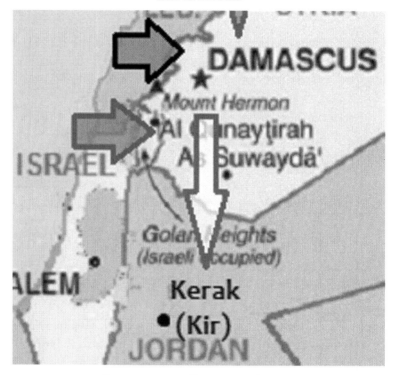

Base map credit: www.cia.gov

Damascus refugees will soon flee to Kerak, Jordan!

By Craig C. White

The Prophet Amos condemned Damascus. He said that God would send an army against Damascus and that the Syrian people would become refugees in Jordan. This prophecy was fulfilled when Tiglath-pileser the Assyrian king conquered Damascus in 734 B.C. and carried the Syrian (Aramean) captives away to Kir. Kir is a mountainous region in western Jordan. However, like many bible prophecies this may also refer to a current event. Today the city of Kir in Jordan is called Kerak. Kerak is in south western Jordan east of the Dead Sea. It has a population of about 20,000. Not including the tens of

35

thousands of Syrian refugees already there. The citizens of Kerak are poor and mostly Christian. By the way Kerak is in the Moab region of Jordan and is very likely where the Judean refugees will flee during Jerusalem's Great Tribulation!

There are about 600,000 Syrian refugees in western Jordan today. This is further evidence that the destruction of Damascus as described in the bible is imminent. It is also evidence that the God of Israel is the one true God and that we all had better heed his word and we had also better humble ourselves before him while there is still time!

In Amos 1:5 below, the plain of Aven is a valley in the northeast part of Lebanon near the Syrian border. Today it is called the Bekaa valley. It has been suggested that Saddam Hussein hid WMD's here before the invasion of Iraq.

Amos 1:3-5 Thus saith the LORD; For three transgressions of Damascus, and for four, I will not turn away the punishment thereof; because they have threshed Gilead with threshing instruments of iron: 4 But I will send a fire into the house of Hazael, which shall devour the palaces of Benhadad. 5 I will break also the bar of Damascus, and cut off the inhabitant from the plain of Aven, and him that holdeth the sceptre from the house of Eden: and the people of Syria shall go into captivity unto Kir, saith the LORD.

God used the terminology to *send a fire* to mean that the Assyrian army would besiege the city. Just as the ancient Assyrians assaulted the city in 734 BC, I think that the Turkish army will do likewise. *The palaces of Benhadad* refer to the thrones of ancient Syrian Kings in Damascus. Like the ancient invasion, this future invasion will also destroy Syria's seat of government in Damascus.

Tens of thousands of Syrians have already taken refuge in Kir (or Kerak) in western Jordan. Many more will join them as Damascus flees. Bible prophecy is coming true. There is a terrible time of Satan's anger and of God's judgment coming on the entire world. It is High Time to surrender your soul into God's care.

Turkey will attack Damascus from the north forcing the Damascus residents to the south towards Jordan. The Damascus residents will take refuge in Kerak, Jordan.

Isaiah 17 and Jeremiah 49 also predict the destruction of Damascus, Syria. They both offer details that can be observed today!

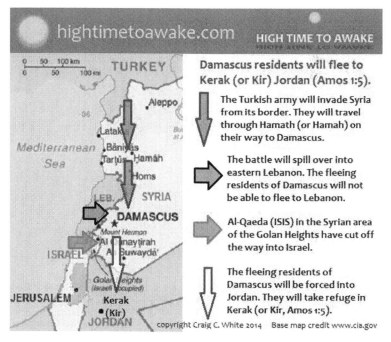

Base map credit: www.cia.gov

Chapter Six

Who is Fighting in Syria?

Free Syrian Army soldier photo credit: Freedom House 2
http://www.flickr.com/

Persia, Ethiopia, and Libya with them

Ezekiel 38:5

By Craig C. White

Ezekiel chapter 38 describes a Middle Eastern invasion into Israel. It is called the battle of Gog and Magog. Most teach that this battle is led by Russia. It is high time to rethink that position. Every nation that is listed in Ezekiel 38 is now fighting in Syria! This battle is led by Turkey! The first phase of the battle of Gog and Magog may begin very soon. Gog is the land of modern Turkey. Magog is its leader.

Ezekiel 38:5 Persia, Ethiopia, and Libya with them; all of them with shield and helmet:

Ezekiel 38:5 above describes the armed forces that will join Turkey in its invasion into Israel. Turkey will be joined by Iran (Persia), Ethiopia/Sudan (The original Hebrew word Cush more accurately describes Sudan), and Libya.

Ezekiel 38:5 also describes an event that is happening now! The Free Syrian Army is fighting against Syrian President Bashar Assad and the Syrian Army. We have all been told that the Syrian citizens are rising up against President Assad. Not true! The Free Syrian Army is made up of mostly Libyans and is fighting to install Muslim Brotherhood leadership in Syria.

Reports are mixed, but the rebel army fighting against Assad and the Syrian army may consist of some 300,000 troops. Their General is Mahdi al-Harati, commander of Libya's Tripoli Brigade. The fighters are not Syrians from Damascus or Aleppo but they are imported jihadists. The Syrian people are working to identify and remove the foreign fighters. In the field the majority of "freedom fighters" are under Turkish command. The fighters are professionals who fought in Afghanistan, Bosnia, Chechnya, or Iraq. The largest contingency of the Free Syrian Army is made up of Al Qaeda terrorists from Libya.

Hezbollah militia from Iran and Sudan are also fighting in Syria against the Free Syrian Army.

Note: Sudan's role in Syria is a little unclear. The fighting in Syria began in the spring of 2011. Early on I heard reports that Hezbollah trained rebel groups from southern Sudan had joined Hezbollah from Iran in the fight in Syria. Hezbollah has had training camps in southern Sudan since 1989. Sudan is predominantly a Sunni Muslim nation. So I have also heard reports that many Sudanese have also joined the opposition groups. Sudan has also been caught supplying weapons to the Sunni opposition groups such as the Free Syrian Army. Even though Sudan is a Sunni nation they have strong economic ties with Iran which is a Shia Muslim nation. So Sudan may be fighting on both sides of the Syrian conflict. It is impossible to know how many Sudanese are fighting in Syria or which side they are on. It may be that Sudan's involvement will become more evident before all of these forces together invade Israel.

In Ezekiel 38:6 below, Gomer and Togarmah are people who settled in today's Turkey. They are joined by "many people" in their invasion into Israel.

Eze 38:6 Gomer, and all his bands; the house of Togarmah of the north quarters, and all his bands: *and many people with thee.*

In Ezekiel 38 Turkey leads the bands from Iran, Sudan, and Libya into Israel. The Turkish army is now conveniently amassed on the Syrian border.

It is my contention that Turkey together with the Free Syrian Army will destroy Damascus as prophesied in Isaiah 17:1 and Jeremiah 49:24-27, and then possibly turn south a few miles into Israel. The stage is now set for the first part of the battle of Gog and Magog described in Ezekiel 38.

It seems that Turkey, the Muslim Brotherhood, and the US want Syria's President Bashar Assad gone! This is an effort to unite the Middle East under the extreme Islamist mantle of the Muslim Brotherhood.

Iran and Sudan are represented in Syria by Hezbollah militia. Hezbollah is pro-Assad and is fighting against "The Free Syrian Army". Lebanon is also pro-Assad and is acting as a base of operations for the Hezbollah militia.

Turkey has the real military power in this fight. Jeremiah 49 predicts the destruction of Damascus, Syria's capital city. I think that Turkey will eventually invade Syria and destroy Damascus.

Copyright 2013 Craig C. White

Who is fighting in Syria - Map

All of the nations mentioned in Ezekiel 38:5 are now fighting in Syria. Ezekiel 38 tells us about an invasion into Israel led by Turkey. This invasion is referred to as the battle of Gog and Magog. Gog is Turkey. Magog is its ruler. Also Isaiah chapter 10 tells us about a future leader who will invade Syria and then invade Israel just like the ancient Assyrians did in 700 BC. I think that after Turkey destroys Damascus they will lead all of the armies listed in Ezekiel 38:5 (Iran, Libya, and Sudan) in an invasion into Israel.

The Turkish led invasion into Israel described in Ezekiel chapter 38 is the major prophetic event of the pre-Tribulation period. It identifies the Antichrist and sets end time events into hyper-drive!

SECTION 2: TURKEY

Turkey is the one nation that causes the most trouble during the end time. Turkey will invade Syria and destroy Damascus. Turkey will invade Israel more than once. Turkey will also conquer Egypt and rule over the next World Empire!

Chapter Seven

Turkey invades Israel!

Syria only the beginning

By Craig C. White

New World Order types have been fighting to unify the Middle East under the mantle of the Muslim Brotherhood. The Muslim Brotherhood briefly had Egypt under its control but lost it. That made them furious. They'll be darned if they allow Syria to slip the grip of Islamist rule. The US has threatened to attack Syria. If that happens then Russia has threatened to attack Saudi Arabia.

Who will attack Syria and destroy Damascus? I think that I will stick to the biblical model for this invasion. In 734 BC the Assyrian empire conquered Syria and then turned immediately south and attacked northern Israel. In 701 BC Assyria returned to attack southern Israel. Do I think that Assyria will attack Syria again? No, but I do think that the man called "the Assyrian" in Isaiah chapter 10 will attack Syria and destroy Damascus. *This Assyrian* isn't from Assyria. The modern day Assyrian is from Turkey.

The bible predicts that Damascus Syria will be destroyed in the last days before a terrible time of God's judgment on earth begins and before the day that Jesus Christ returns to defeat Israel's enemies.

Isa 17:1 The burden of Damascus. Behold, Damascus is taken away from *being* a city, and it shall be a ruinous heap.

The Destruction of Damascus is a prophecy that at first glance seems to stand alone but it turns out that it is only the first in a sequence of even more dramatic and telling events. Ezekiel chapter 38 tells us about a Turkish led invasion into Israel. Turkey is accompanied by Iran, Sudan, and Libya (Ezekiel 38:5). Saudi Arabia is also mentioned in

Ezekiel 38:13. Guess what? All of these nations are fighting in Syria today! Plus the Turkish army is aligned along the Syria border. The scene is set for the Ezekiel 38 battle of Gog and Magog. I know that Magog is a strange word but he is one of Noah's grandsons. He is described as the most prominent prince amongst his brothers (Ezekiel 38:2). Today Magog represents the "primary governor" of Turkey. I would call him the Prime Minister of Turkey. Turkish Prime Minister Erdogan is the modern day fulfillment of Magog in Ezekiel 38. I think that he is also the fulfillment of the Assyrian in Isaiah 10.

After the destruction of Damascus, Turkish Prime Minister Erdogan will lead Al-Qaeda terrorists from Libya and also Hezbollah jihadists from Iran and Sudan in an invasion into Israel. As if this wasn't bad enough, the bible identifies the leader of this invasion as the Antichrist. To put a little more fire under your britches, the revealing of the Antichrist is the sign that the Rapture of the Church is eminent!

More from High Time to Awake

Available from Amazon.com, CreateSpace.com, and other retail outlets. Also available on Kindle and other devices.

Turkey invades Israel - Halfway to Armageddon alerts us to a coming invasion into Israel led by Turkey! It is called the battle of Gog and Magog in Ezekiel chapter 38. You probably don't realize that you need to know all there is about the battle of Gog and Magog, but trust me this subject is about to define our time in biblical history! The Turkish led battle of *Gog and Magog* is the fulfillment of **the preeminent** pre-Tribulation bible prophecy!

www.hightimetoawake.com

SECTION 3: SUDAN

Sudan plays an active role in the end time. Sudan follows Turkey as it invades Israel and Egypt. Today Hezbollah fighters from Sudan are fighting in Syria. Sudan is referred to as *Ethiopia* in the English King James Bible.

Chapter Eight

Ethiopia is Sudan!

Ezekiel 38:5

By Craig C. White

We are told about an end time Turkish led invasion into Israel in Ezekiel 38. *Persia, Ethiopia, and Libya* will join Turkey in this invasion. Most folks know that *Persia* is the ancient name for today's Iran. *Libya* is easily identified as today's Libya. But when it comes to identifying *Ethiopia* we may falter. It seems obvious at first but the English translation is somewhat misleading. The English translators chose a convenient title for their day but the nation of Ethiopia didn't exist at the time that Ezekiel wrote his prophecy!

Ezekiel 38:5 Persia, Ethiopia, and Libya with them; all of them with shield and helmet:

The name *Ethiopia* is only as old as about 400 AD. That name was given long after Ezekiel wrote his prophecy (Ezekiel 38:5)! The name Ethiopia comes from the Greek word "Aethiopia" referring to the people who lived south of Egypt. The original Hebrew word translated as "Ethiopia" in the English bible is the Hebrew word "Cush". Look it up in your concordance! Cush was one of Noah's grandsons who settled the land south of Egypt (Genesis 10, 1Chronicles 1). Sudan is the major nation today that is located directly south of Egypt. Ethiopia is southeast of Sudan. When you read "Ethiopia" in the English bible you can be certain that it is referring to the modern day nation of *Sudan*!

By the way all of these nations are represented in the forces fighting in Syria today! It seems likely that after the destruction of Damascus, Syria that these armies will turn south into Israel led by Turkey! It is High Time to Awake!

SECTION 4: EGYPT

Egypt was taken over by the Islamist Muslim Brotherhood. Somehow they were able to escape their grip. The bible tells us that the Antichrist will eventually conquer Egypt. The bible says that in the end Egypt shall not escape! I think that Turkey will invade Egypt probably during the seven year Tribulation period!

Chapter Nine

The Burden of Egypt

Photo credit: jay8085
http://www.flickr.com/

Pucker up your Sphinx!

A verse by verse study through Isaiah chapter 19

By Craig C. White

Isaiah 19 tells us about "the burden of Egypt" in the last days. The burden of Egypt is the trouble that God will afflict upon them for their unbelief and hostility towards Israel. The Egyptian nation hasn't been all bad, and neither is their fate. They will suffer seriously, but they will also be restored. Egypt took in Jacob and his family in time of drought, and preserved the nation of Israel (Gen 45). Of course they later enslaved the Hebrews, and God judged them. Christianity was the majority religion in Egypt during the 4th to 6th centuries. In 1965 Egyptian president Nasser said "Our basic objective will be the destruction of Israel. The Arab people want to fight." which led to the six day war. Egypt attacked Israel again in 1973 during the Yom Kippur war. In 1979 Egypt and Israel brokered a peace agreement, and have kept it until now. Until recently Egypt has hosted the Coptic Christians and has been at peace with Israel. But in the past few years Egypt has persecuted and killed the Coptic Christians, and has turned against Israel. Their latest President Mohamed Morsi is determined to place a Palestinian state inside the land of Israel. The events described in Isaiah 19 happen around the time of Jesus Christ's second coming. Some of these events seem to be happening already!

Isa 19:1 The burden of Egypt. Behold, the LORD rideth upon a swift cloud, and shall come into Egypt: and the idols of Egypt shall be moved at his presence, and the heart of Egypt shall melt in the midst of it.

Jesus will swoop down into Egypt at his second coming. Many Christians think that Jesus will descend out of heaven and immediately stand on the mount of olives (Zec 14:4), but I think that God will first bring his son out of Egypt (Num 24:8-9)! Please read my commentary titled "Revelation Wrath Path" in my book "Israel's Beacon of Hope".

Isa 19:2 And I will set the Egyptians against the Egyptians: and they shall fight every one against his brother, and every one against his neighbour; city against city, *and* kingdom against kingdom. 3 And the spirit of Egypt shall fail in the midst thereof; and I will destroy the counsel thereof: and they shall seek to the idols, and to the charmers, and to them that have familiar spirits, and to the wizards.

Today we are seeing Egyptians fighting against Egyptians. It seems that half of all Egyptians are protesting their ex-ruler Morsi and the Muslim Brotherhood as they grapple for absolute authority. The other half supports the Muslim Brotherhood and is terrorizing the country. Supporters of ousted Egyptian President Mohamed Morsi are being helped by the Muslim Brotherhood. As you know the protests are becoming more violent. Coptic Christians in Egypt are being persecuted more and more.

Lately Saudi Arabia has been working with the Egyptian interim government and are curtailing Muslim Brotherhood activities.

Isa 19:4 And the Egyptians will I give over into the hand of a cruel lord; and a fierce king shall rule over them, saith the Lord, the LORD of hosts.

Speaking of *cruel lord*; Egyptian ex-President Mohamed Morsi was Egypt's first Islamist president. He is a member of the Muslim Brotherhood. Morsi believes in establishing an Islamic state in Egypt and also in Israel. He is trying to take complete control of the nation of Egypt. It is possible that Egypt has had its cruel lord! Morsi is being imprisoned today in an Egyptian army barracks. There have already been break out attempts made by the Muslim Brotherhood. It is possible that we haven't seen the last of him. It is possible that President Morsi is Egypt's cruel lord!

I suspect that another ruler may fulfill the position of Egypt's *fierce king*. But I'm not certain. The Saudi royal family is heavily involved in the reorganization of the Egyptian government and its law. Perhaps Egypt's *fierce king* will come from Saudi Arabia. I think that Egypt's ex-President Morsi may yet make a comeback. Morsi may in fact be the rotten ruler that Egypt should expect. Ultimately I think that Egypt will fall under the military might of Turkey but that is another story.

Isa 19:5 And the waters shall fail from the sea, and the river shall be wasted and dried up. 6a And they shall turn the rivers far away; *and* **the brooks of defence shall be emptied and dried up:**

God will dry up the Nile River! Today Ethiopia and Sudan are beginning to use a lot more of the Nile's water. Several foreign countries and large agricultural companies are leasing huge tracts of land to grow crops. Ethiopia has plans to build a huge hydroelectric dam. So much less water will be reaching the Egyptian shores downstream. I'm sure that this is all just coincidence.

Isa 19:6b the reeds and flags shall wither. 7 The paper reeds by the brooks, by the mouth of the brooks, and every thing sown by the brooks, shall wither, be driven away, and be no *more.* **8 The fishers also shall mourn, and all they that cast angle into the brooks shall lament, and they that spread nets upon the waters shall languish. 9 Moreover they that work in fine flax, and they that weave networks, shall be confounded. 10 And they shall be broken in the purposes thereof, all that make sluices** *and* **ponds for fish.**

Everything that grows along the Nile River will die. The Nile River supports most of the population living along it. Those folks will lose their way of making a living. Fishing in the Nile will cease. Flax will no longer grow along the Nile. Flax is used to make fine linen. The entire nation will become impoverished.

Isa 19:11 Surely the princes of Zoan *are* **fools, the counsel of the wise counsellors of Pharaoh is become brutish: how say ye unto Pharaoh, I** *am* **the son of the wise, the son of ancient kings? 12 Where** *are* **they? where** *are* **thy wise** *men?* **and let them tell thee now, and let them know what the LORD of hosts hath purposed upon Egypt. 13 The princes of Zoan are become fools, the princes of Noph are deceived; they have also seduced Egypt,** *even they that are* **the stay of the tribes**

thereof. 14 The LORD hath mingled a perverse spirit in the midst thereof: and they have caused Egypt to err in every work thereof, as a drunken *man* staggereth in his vomit. 15 Neither shall there be *any* work for Egypt, which the head or tail, branch or rush, may do.

Zoan is a city in the Nile delta. Noph is the Hebrew name for the ancient Egyptian city of Memphis. It is near Cairo today. Verses 11-14 above are saying that the Egyptian leadership will make stupid decisions. Every idea that they have will result in further ruin. Today top Muslim clerics are urging the destruction of the Egyptian pyramids, Sphinx, and other non Islamist monuments. That sounds like a bad idea to me. Egypt's tourism is already devastated due to protests. Destroying Egypt's monuments would eradicate tourism to Egypt forever in one day. Egypt will be left without industry or livelihood.

Isa 19:16 In that day shall Egypt be like unto women: and it shall be afraid and fear because of the shaking of the hand of the LORD of hosts, which he shaketh over it. 17 And the land of Judah shall be a terror unto Egypt, every one that maketh mention thereof shall be afraid in himself, because of the counsel of the LORD of hosts, which he hath determined against it.

Egypt will fear southern Israel with whom they share a border. Judah is southern Israel including Jerusalem. Because of Egypt's worsening condition, the Egyptian people will realize that the God of Israel has it in for them. Perhaps they will read Isaiah 19.

Isa 19:18 In that day shall five cities in the land of Egypt speak the language of Canaan, and swear to the LORD of hosts; one shall be called, The city of destruction. 19 In that day shall there be an altar to the LORD in the midst of the land of Egypt, and a pillar at the border thereof to the LORD. 20 And it shall be for a sign and for a witness unto the LORD of hosts in the land of Egypt: for they shall cry unto the LORD

because of the oppressors, and he shall send them a saviour, and a great one, and he shall deliver them. 21 And the LORD shall be known to Egypt, and the Egyptians shall know the LORD in that day, and shall do sacrifice and oblation; yea, they shall vow a vow unto the LORD, and perform *it.*

After Egypt's time of trouble the people will turn to the God of Israel! I don't think that the word "savior" in Isaiah 19:20 refers to Jesus. But Jesus will send another person to Egypt to deliver the people from their tyrannical leadership. I think that these events happen sometime after Jesus returns and sets up his throne in Jerusalem.

Isa 19:22 And the LORD shall smite Egypt: he shall smite and heal *it:* **and they shall return** *even* **to the LORD, and he shall be intreated of them, and shall heal them.**

Isaiah 19:22 summarizes the entire 19th chapter of Isaiah. Now let me summarize Isaiah 19:22. Egypt will suffer seriously, but then they will be restored.

Isa 19:23 In that day shall there be a highway out of Egypt to Assyria, and the Assyrian shall come into Egypt, and the Egyptian into Assyria, and the Egyptians shall serve with the Assyrians. 24 In that day shall Israel be the third with Egypt and with Assyria, *even* **a blessing in the midst of the land: 25 Whom the LORD of hosts shall bless, saying, Blessed** *be* **Egypt my people, and Assyria the work of my hands, and Israel mine inheritance.**

Assyria is best represented today by northern Iraq. Guess what? This represents the land area that God originally gave to Abraham! God will keep his promise!

Gen 15:18 In the same day the LORD made a covenant with Abram, saying, Unto thy seed have I given this land, from the river of Egypt unto the great river, the river Euphrates:

More from High Time to Awake

Available from Amazon.com, CreateSpace.com, and other retail outlets. Also available on Kindle and other devices.

Just before Israel's seven year period of Tribulation the nations in the old world will fight against one another.

Luke 21:10 Then said he unto them, Nation shall rise against nation, and kingdom against kingdom:

Nation by Nation Verse by Verse identifies a few key nations who will play significant roles during the years leading up to and during Israel's time of trouble. We will take a verse by verse look at specific prophetic events that these nations will fulfill. I expect that these prophecies reflect the near time future of world history.

Chapter Ten

There shall be a highway out of Egypt.

Photo credit: David Evers
http://www.flickr.com/

Rivers into Roadways

Isaiah 19:23

By Craig C. White

There are some good things and some bad things said about Egypt in Bible Prophecy. Isaiah 19 is about Egypt during the time period after Jesus Christ returns to earth. It is a fascinating read. Egypt will be ruled by a cruel leader and will suffer greatly. Read about Egypt's Cruel Lord in Isaiah 19 (The Burden of Egypt). Eventually Egypt will turn to Jesus and their nation will be healed. They will serve the Lord along with Assyria. The Assyrian empire was headquartered in the city of Nineveh. Nineveh today is in northern Iraq. Traces of Its walls can still be seen. In the days after the tribulation there will be a highway from Egypt to Iraq.

Isa 19:23 In that day shall there be a highway out of Egypt to Assyria, and the Assyrian shall come into

Egypt, and the Egyptian into Assyria, and the Egyptians shall serve with the Assyrians.

Guess what? There is a highway from Egypt to Iraq today! As a matter of fact there are several. So it seems to me that we are prepared for the return of Jesus Christ. Yup, there is a highway from Egypt to Iraq. However, during the final gathering of Jews to Israel that highway will be under further construction.

In Egypt God will dry up the Gulf of Aqaba on the Red Sea. He will also dry up the Nile River. God will also dry up the Euphrates and Tigris rivers in order to make a way to cross over them. Just like the day that God parted the Red Sea to let the Hebrews cross over; God will again put Egypt on the bible road-atlas!

The Hebrew word Aliyah literally means ascent. Aliyah is the immigration of Jews to the Land of Israel. When Jesus returns to earth after the tribulation, Jews will be raised from the dead and return to the land of Israel by the hundreds of millions. To accommodate all those travelers God will provide a highway from Egypt to Northern Iraq. God will also make some improvements along the way. The return of believing Jews to Israel is going to be first rate!

When Jesus returns he will raise the dead to life! At that time all faithful persons of ancient Israel will be resurrected (Dan 12:13)! Many of them were scattered to other countries so they will need to be brought back to their own land. The ancient Jews will ascend from the grave and then ascend back to their land.

Isa 11:11-12 And it shall come to pass in that day, *that* the Lord shall set his hand again the second time to recover the remnant of his people, which shall be left, from Assyria, and from Egypt, and from Pathros, and from Cush, and from Elam, and from Shinar, and from Hamath, and from the islands of the sea. 12 And he

shall set up an ensign for the nations, and shall assemble the outcasts of Israel, and gather together the dispersed of Judah from the four corners of the earth.

Note: In Isaiah 11:11-12 (above) Assyria is northern Iraq, Egypt is the Sinai peninsula, Pathros is upper Egypt, Cush is Ethiopia, Elam is Iran, Shinar is southern Iraq, and Hamath means citadel (see the citadel at Shushan, or modern Shush in western Iran). I think it refers to Israel's captivity under Persia (Iran). Remember some Jews remained under captivity after Babylon was conquered by the Medes and Persians, including Daniel the prophet.

The nation of Israel was taken captive first in Egypt, then Assyria, and then Babylon. Of course they have also been dispersed into all corners of the world. Well, God wants them back. Jesus will raise-up these captives and bring them back to the land of Israel! To do this he will need to make some improvements to the roadways.

Isa 11:15-16 And the LORD shall utterly destroy the tongue of the Egyptian sea; and with his mighty wind shall he shake his hand over the river, and shall smite it in the seven streams, and make *men* go over dryshod. 16 And there shall be an highway for the remnant of his people, which shall be left, from Assyria; like as it was to Israel in the day that he came up out of the land of Egypt.

God prepares a highway for the resurrected Hebrews to return to Israel. In Isaiah (above) Jesus dries up the Gulf of Aqaba on the Red Sea (that is *the tongue of the Egyptian sea*)! He will also dry up the Nile, Euphrates, and Tigris rivers in order to make a way to cross over them. Won't that be nice for the ancient captives? One day they will be raised from the dead, and the next day they will be crossing the Red Sea just like Moses did! That sounds like a fun packed weekend. Drying up rivers seems to be God's preferred method of providing highways. By the way Moses will only need to cross the Jordan River on that day.

Moses was buried in today's Jordan, just east of Israel (Deu 34:6).

Here are some more verses about turning rivers into roadways.

Isa 27:12-13 And it shall come to pass in that day, *that* the LORD shall beat off from the channel of the river unto the stream of Egypt, and ye shall be gathered one by one, O ye children of Israel. 13 And it shall come to pass in that day, *that* the great trumpet shall be blown, and they shall come which were ready to perish in the land of Assyria, and the outcasts in the land of Egypt, and shall worship the LORD in the holy mount at Jerusalem.

In Zechariah (below) "*the pride of Assyria*" is the Tigris River, and "*the sceptre of Egypt*" is the Nile River. God will gather the ancient Jewish captives to southwestern Syria (Gilead) and Lebanon until there is no more room! I am guessing that the highway described in Isa 19:23 (at the top of this commentary) runs from Egypt near Gaza, up the Mediterranean coast through Israel, into Lebanon, then turns due east through Syria, and runs all the way to Nineveh in northern Iraq. That's my guess, you had better check with AAA before making the trip!

Zec 10:10-12 I will bring them again also out of the land of Egypt, and gather them out of Assyria; and I will bring them into the land of Gilead and Lebanon; and *place* shall not be found for them. 11 And he shall pass through the sea with affliction, and shall smite the waves in the sea, and all the deeps of the river shall dry up: and the pride of Assyria shall be brought down, and the sceptre of Egypt shall depart away. 12 And I will strengthen them in the LORD; and they shall walk up and down in his name, saith the LORD.

Jeremiah chapter 31 (below) is written to the northern kingdom of Israel which was taken captive to Assyria. The northern kingdom was headquartered in the land of the tribe of Ephraim in Samaria, north of Jerusalem. Jeremiah speaks of Israel and Ephraim in chapter 31; the Hebrew captives of Assyria have been raised from the dead and are walking back to Israel. In the verse below "*waymarks*" and "*high heaps*" are road markers. The Aliyah highway wouldn't be complete without street signs!

Jer 31:21 Set thee up waymarks, make thee high heaps: set thine heart toward the highway, *even* the way *which* thou wentest: turn again, O virgin of Israel, turn again to these thy cities.

God will prepare the way for Israel to return (aliyah) to their land. Even so Israel aliyah, arise return!

Chapter Eleven

Egypt shall not escape

The Antichrist will invade Egypt then Israel.

Daniel 11:40-45

By Craig C. White

There is a movement in Northern Africa and the Middle East to bring the region under an Islamist umbrella. Egypt has loosed the bands of the Muslim Brotherhood for now, but ultimately Egypt will not escape. During the first half of the seven year Tribulation period Turkey will conquer Egypt!

Antiochus Epiphanies was the king over one quarter of the Grecian Empire headquartered in Syria. Antiochus Epiphanies is a forerunner and type of the Antichrist. The Antichrist will do many of the same things that Antiochus Epiphanies did.

Ezekiel 39:1 identifies the Prime Minister (*chief prince*) of Turkey as the future invader of Israel. Ezekiel chapter 39 describes the battle of Armageddon led by the Antichrist. So a Turkish Prime Minister will be the Antichrist. The battle of Armageddon happens at the end of the seven year Tribulation period.

Daniel chapter 11 describes an invasion into Egypt and then into Israel that happened in 167 BC led by Antiochus Epiphanies. I think that Daniel chapter 11 also predicts a future invasion of Egypt and then Israel led by the Antichrist. This isn't the battle of Armageddon. Instead it is the attack that begins the Great Tribulation (Mat 24:21). This invasion into Egypt and then Israel happens in the middle of the seven year Tribulation period. In Daniel 11 below, the king of the south is Egypt. The king of the north is Turkey in this future invasion into Egypt and then into Israel!

Dan 11:40 And at the time of the end shall the king of the south push at him: and the king of the north shall come against him like a whirlwind, with chariots, and with horsemen, and with many ships; and he shall enter into the countries, and shall overflow and pass over. 41 He shall enter also into the glorious land, and many *countries* shall be overthrown: but these shall escape out of his hand, *even* Edom, and Moab, and the chief of the children of Ammon.

So Turkey will invade Egypt and even come into Israel (*the glorious land*). It sounds like Turkey will conquer all of Northern Africa and the Middle East except for Jordan. *Edom*, *Moab*, and *Ammon* all represent today's Jordan.

Dan 11:42 He shall stretch forth his hand also upon the countries: and the land of Egypt shall not escape. 43 But he shall have power over the treasures of gold and of silver, and over all the precious things of Egypt: and the Libyans and the Ethiopians *shall be* at his steps.

The Antichrist (Turkish Prime Minister) will loot Egypt of its treasures. Turkey will be joined in its conquests by Libya and Sudan.

Dan 11:44 But tidings out of the east and out of the north shall trouble him: therefore he shall go forth with great fury to destroy, and utterly to make away many.

Remember that this account refers to two separate invasions of Egypt and then Israel. In 167 BC Antiochus Epiphanies heard news of a Jewish effort to take control of the temple in Jerusalem. He then invaded Israel to stop it. Turkey will invade Egypt in the future led by the Antichrist. He will probably also hear news from Jerusalem concerning the newly built temple.

Here is a historical account of Antiochus Epiphanies' attack on Israel in 167 BC. The Turkish Antichrist will attack Israel in much the same way.

2 Maccabees 5:11–14 When these happenings were reported to the king, he thought that Judea was in revolt. Raging like a wild animal, he set out from Egypt and took Jerusalem by storm. He ordered his soldiers to cut down without mercy those whom they met and to slay those who took refuge in their houses. There was a massacre of young and old, a killing of women and children, a slaughter of virgins and infants. In the space of three days, eighty thousand were lost, forty thousand meeting a violent death, and the same number being sold into slavery.

Dan 11:45 And he shall plant the tabernacles of his palace between the seas in the glorious holy mountain; yet he shall come to his end, and none shall help him.

The *seas* described in this verse are typically thought to be the Mediterranean Sea and the Dead Sea. Jerusalem is between the two seas. The glorious holy mountain is Mt. Zion in Jerusalem. In 167 BC Antiochus Epiphanies took-over the temple in Jerusalem and declared that he should be worshiped as god. In the future the Antichrist will also take-over the temple in Jerusalem and declare that he should be worshiped there. This verse reflects the desecration of the temple spoken of in Dan 12:11 and referenced in Mat 24:15-16. When the Jews around Jerusalem see the Antichrist claiming to be god in the temple at Jerusalem then they are instructed to flee to the hills of Jordan!

In the middle of the Tribulation the Antichrist will attack Israel. This begins Jerusalem's *Great Tribul*ation (Mat 24:21)! Just before his armies invade Israel they will invade Egypt and carry away their treasures. So when Israel sees Turkey invade Egypt they will have an advanced warning that they will be attacked next!

Today Egypt has seemingly avoided a Muslim Brotherhood takeover but in the end the entire Middle East and northern Africa will be under the control of the Antichrist.

PS: Daniel chapter 11 doesn't describe the other Turkish led invasion into Israel that is described in Ezekiel chapter 38. Turkey will first invade Syria and destroy Damascus. Then Turkey will lead Iran, Sudan, and Libya into Israel. All of these forces are fighting in Syria today! I think that this invasion could begin shortly!

More from High Time to Awake

Available from Amazon.com, CreateSpace.com, and other retail outlets. Also available on Kindle and other devices.

High Time to Awake **Highlights** contains a collection of my best bible prophecy commentaries. I chose these commentaries to be among my best based on their urgency of message, their timeliness, their carefulness of research, the attention given in writing them, their helpfulness to understanding end time prophecy, and also for the scarcity of these views being shared elsewhere. I hope these commentaries give you a solid foundation of understanding for our times, and also a clearer awareness of God's presence in your life.

www.hightimetoawake.com

SECTION 5: RUSSIA

Today the news is filled with stories about Russia taking back territory along its western border. 2,600 years ago the Prophet Daniel told us all about it. According to Daniel a new Russian Union will be part of the next world empire.

Also Russia may play the role of military police in Israel during the second half of the Tribulation period.

Rev 13:2 And the beast which I saw was like unto a leopard, and his feet were as *the feet* of a bear, and his mouth as the mouth of a lion: and the dragon gave him his power, and his seat, and great authority.

The "beast" in Revelation and Daniel are both identifying the next world empire.

Dan 7:19 Then I would know the truth of the fourth beast, which was diverse from all the others, exceeding dreadful, whose teeth *were of* iron, and his nails *of* brass; *which* devoured, brake in pieces, and stamped the residue with his feet;

The feet of the beast represent Russia. The *residue* in the verse above may describe the few remaining Jews left inside of the land of Israel during the Great Tribulation.

More from High Time to Awake

Available from Amazon.com, CreateSpace.com, and other retail outlets. Also available on Kindle and other devices.

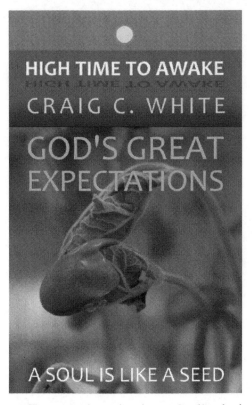

God's Great Expectations is about God's desire to know us, and about the ramifications of knowing him or rejecting him. It will challenge and inform every Christian. It answers the question "who can be saved?" It also contains an in-depth definition of hell in the bible, and a map of heaven! In "God's Great Expectations" I cover Jesus' claims to be God, as well as the Rapture of the Church.

www.hightimetoawake.com

Chapter Twelve

Caution! Russia in Bible Prophecy

© 2013 Craig C. White

From my house I can't see Russia!

By Craig C. White

The new Russian Union is here! Kazakhstan and Belarus have joined Russia in a new Eurasian economic Union. I think this is a big step. Daniel chapter 7 tells us about the Russian bear during the end times. If the three ribs in Daniel 7:5 represent nations along Russia's western border then two of them are represented here. This is a new Russian Union! Christians should be alerted that Daniel 7 is moving forward. This is an economic Union. I expect that three nations will one day soon say to Russia, You must create a Political Union!

Somehow the Russian place in bible prophecy is compelling. But too often we see bears where there are none. We also overlook the bears that are there. The Russian bear will have its place in end time prophecy, but it probably isn't what you thought. Hey, I see a bear! Where? Over there!

A lot of folks say that Russia will lead an invasion into Israel as Described in Ezekiel chapter 38. I don't see Russia in Ezekiel 38 (Gog and Magog). That view came about by transcribing "chief" (or the Hebrew "rosh") to mean Russia. Rosh means first or primary. Transposing Hebrew words into English phonetic equivalents is not proper interpretive technique, and is not used elsewhere. Gog is the land of modern Turkey and Magog is its leader or at least its chief founder.

I do however see Russia in Daniel chapter 7.

Dan 7:5 And behold another beast, a second, like to a bear, and it raised up itself on one side, and *it had* three ribs in the mouth of it between the teeth of it: and they said thus unto it, Arise, devour much flesh.

The nation that is obviously symbolized by a bear is Russia. For the last one hundred years prophecy scholars have identified the bear in the prophecy of Daniel 7 as Russia. The bear has three ribs in its mouth. I think the three ribs are yet to come. But let me alert you! We are already seeing signs of them! They are in (or among) the teeth like a bit. They exist together at the same time. They speak to the bear all at once. They may be Russian political or military leaders or perhaps the ribs are nations adjacent to Russia. I think the bear is devouring (or eating) territory. I think the Russian bear is raised up along its southwestern border to bring back under its authority (and ultimately into the fold of the revived World Empire) the following countries: Georgia, Armenia, and Azerbaijan all north of the Caucasus Mountains; also Belarus, Ukraine, and Moldova all west of the Ural Mountains. Most people will tell you that the Roman Empire didn't extend into Russia, but the best scholarship says that it reached as far as the western slopes of the Ural Mountains. In 2008 Russia tested its ability to take back the former Soviet territory of Georgia.

In Daniel chapter 7 the bear represents Russia. As a prelude to the final gentile world empire Russia will gain territory along its southwestern border. Russia has been active in this process for the last twenty years. My guess is that we will soon see a dramatic culmination of this process. A security alliance called the CSTO was signed into force in May 1992. It includes Russia, Armenia, Belarus, Kazakhstan, Kyrgyzstan, Tajikistan and Uzbekistan. In Russian President Medvedev's state of the union address in Dec 2011 he proclaimed Russia's intentions of a Eurasian Economic Union. Russia also has aggressive economic alliances with Belarus and Kazakhstan.

For more about Russia in Bible Prophecy read my commentary on Daniel chapter 7 titled "The Leopard is Upon Us!" in my book The Fall of Satan and Rise of the Antichrist. It is one of my most important bible prophecy commentaries.

Chapter Thirteen

Russia to Invade!?

Russia will conquer several countries along its western border!

By Craig C. White

Russia will conquer several countries along its western border! OK folks. I have been saying this for years, but you have been reluctant to believe me. Well now everybody is saying that Russia is about to invade Ukraine along with Belarus, Georgia and other nations along its western border. I'm not an expert in world politics. So how did I predict this? I read about it in Daniel Chapter 7. If you want to know what is going to happen next according to end time bible prophecy then read my "High Time to Awake" commentaries! And please trust me just a little!

Many bible prophecy students expect Russia to invade Israel. I don't. Russia will invade another country; however this may not be the invasion that you expect!

Dan 7:5 And behold another beast, a second, like to a bear, and it raised up itself on one side, and *it had* three ribs in the mouth of it between the teeth of it: and they said thus unto it, Arise, devour much flesh.

The nation that is obviously symbolized by a bear is Russia. For the last one hundred years prophecy scholars have identified the bear in Daniel 7 as Russia. I think the three ribs are yet to come. But let me alert you! We are already seeing signs of them! They are in (or among) the teeth like a bit. They exist together at the same time. They speak to the bear all at once. They may be Russian political or military leaders or the ribs may be nations aligned with Russia. I think they are devouring (or eating) territory. I think the Russian bear is raised up along its southwestern border to bring back under its authority (and ultimately into the fold of the revived Roman Empire) the following countries: Georgia, Armenia, and Azerbaijan all north of the Caucasus Mountains; also Belarus, Ukraine, and Moldova all west of the Ural Mountains. Most people will tell you that the Roman Empire didn't extend into Russia, but the best scholarship says that it reached as far as the western slopes of the Ural Mountains. In 2008 Russia tested its ability to take back the former Soviet territory of Georgia.

The nations that Russia is likely to conquer are the nations that were part of the ancient Roman Empire and also former Soviet Union territories but not part of the European Union or Middle East. Remember, the goal is to reconstitute the territories of the ancient Roman Empire.

Russia will conquer several countries along its western border. This is happening now! I think that the destruction of Damascus, Syria by Turkey could be the catalyst to speed up the formation of Russia's new Union.

Chapter Fourteen

Russia vs Ukraine

Three nations call for a new Russian Union

By Craig C. White

Folks seem to be stirred up over the possibility of a Russian takeover of Ukraine. The other possibility is a European takeover of Ukraine. Add to the instability in Ukraine another close neighbor and ally to Russia. Syria is about to fall to Islamist factions. Justifiably Russia is feeling nervous about its western border. I would like to point out that Ukraine has been aligned with Russia up to now. Russia has several major oil pipelines that run through Ukraine to Europe. I am certain that Russia will not relinquish control of Ukraine to western powers.

Will the US get involved in Ukraine? I don't think so. First of all it would be difficult to defend Ukraine against Russia from afar; and defend it for whom? Second consider this. The US has supported the Islamist rebels in Syria. Russia has supported Syrian President Assad and has threatened the US against involvement in Syria. The region is being divided into an Islamist Middle East, Russian states, and Central Asian states. The US may concede Ukraine to Russia in exchange for more latitude in Syria. That being said we may now expect a more aggressive offensive in Syria. In bible prophecy terms that may mean the soon destruction of Damascus.

Ukraine is a prior Soviet bloc nation and the largest country on Russia's western border. There is a political battle going on in Ukraine. Half of its citizens want to align the country with the European Union and the other half want to align with Russia. Pro-EU protestors have taken to the streets in violence after Ukraine President Viktor Yanukovych signed an economic agreement with Russia. Lately protestors have taken over the Presidential office and residence in Kiev sending President Yanukovych fleeing for safety. Now it seems that an unstable Ukraine is up for grabs to the European Union or to Russia. My bet is that Russia wants Ukraine much more and that Russia has the power to get their way.

Does the bible say anything about the fate of Ukraine? Well not by name but I think that it does spell out the formation of an end time Russian Union including its neighbors along its western border.

More from High Time to Awake

Available from Amazon.com, CreateSpace.com, and other retail outlets. Also available on Kindle and other devices.

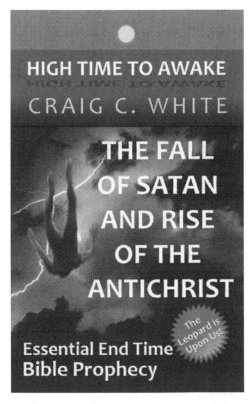

The Fall of Satan and Rise of the Antichrist explains how the Antichrist is the sign of the Rapture. This book contains "The Leopard is Upon Us!" about the formation of the final gentile world empire. It also looks at Mystery Babylon from a fly's eye view.

www.hightimetoawake.com

SECTION 6: UNITED STATES

Is the United State mentioned in Bible Prophecy? I think that it is but it isn't mentioned very much. The symbol of the United States is the eagle but not all eagles in the bible represent the United States.

I have encountered several bible teachers that teach that Mystery Babylon is the United States. Please allow me to tell you that the U.S. definitely is not Mystery Babylon! First of all Revelation tells us that Mystery Babylon is a city.

Rev 17:18 And the woman which thou sawest is that great city,

Mystery Babylon is also a wealthy seaport town that imports a lot of luxury goods (Rev 18:17-19).

The United States may be mentioned in Daniel 7:4 as *eagle's wings*. They are described as participating in the formation of the next World Empire.

Chapter Fifteen

The US in bible prophecy

By Craig C. White

A High Time to Awake reader asked, "Why don't you emphasize the US in bible prophecy?"

The US certainly is playing a role in end time events. They are facilitating the Islamic takeover of the Middle East. They are also allowing the formation of a growing Russian Union. Also their stand with Israel is weak. The US is working to create a Palestinian State inside of Israel. John Kerry may be playing the role of the *hired shepherd* in John 10:11-13. Bible Prophecy emphasizes the old world nations of Northern Egypt, the Middle East, and central Asia. The US is not emphasized in the bible.

I do see the US represented as the *eagle's wings* in Daniel 7:4.

Dan 7:4 The first was like a lion, and had eagle's wings: I beheld till the wings thereof were plucked, and it was lifted up from the earth, and made stand upon the feet as a man, and a man's heart was given to it.

In Daniel chapter 7 the lion with eagle's wings is one of three groups of nations (or Unions) that combine to form the next World Empire. The symbol of England is a lion with eagle's wings. I think that the US assists a British ruler in negotiating the next World Empire. Perhaps the British ruler will represent the European Union or perhaps the British ruler and the United States will represent NATO of which they are both members?

Chapter Sixteen

The Hired Shepherd

Photo credit: by Flavio www.flickr.com

rent-a tender

John 10:11-13

By Craig C. White

Did you know that the verse below (John 10:11-13) is prophetic? The security of Israel will be turned over to others. A leader will be hired to ensure the safety of the Israeli people. He is called the *hired shepherd*. He will not care for the people because they are not his. The people will reject him. I don't think that the hired shepherd is the same person as the Antichrist. The Antichrist will enforce a security agreement upon Israel (Dan 9:27). It may be that another will be hired to administer it. Also Israel's own leaders will allow this to happen (Eze 34:2). God will raise one leader in particular who will sell his people for his own profit. He is Israeli. He is called the *idol shepherd* in Zec 11:16-17. The idol shepherd is a leader who does not care for his own sheepfold. The sheepfold is Israel. Jesus is their true shepherd. At the end of the tribulation he will call them home.

John 10:11-13 I am the good shepherd: the good shepherd giveth his life for the sheep. 12 But he that is an hireling, and not the shepherd, whose own the sheep are not, seeth the wolf coming, and leaveth the sheep, and fleeth: and the wolf catcheth them, and scattereth the sheep. 13 The hireling fleeth, because he is an hireling, and careth not for the sheep.

The hired shepherd is non-Israeli. The idol shepherd is Israeli. I think that both of these leaders could rule at the same time. The hired shepherd will be a non-Jewish leader. It is high time to awake and watch for leaders in Israel who will turn their nation's security over to a hireling!

US Secretary of State John Kerry is leading the charge for the creation of a Palestinian State inside of Israel. Palestinian peace negotiators want Israel to remove their military. Kerry has suggested that US troops should be placed inside of Israel as peacekeepers. It seems to me that US Secretary of State John Kerry is playing the role of the *hired shepherd* today.

.

Chapter Seventeen

Photo credit: by Peter G. Trimming www.flickr.com

Bible verses about Eagles Wings

Wait, don't forget your wings!

Isaiah 40:31

By Craig C. White

Eagle's wings do not always represent the United States in the bible! Here are some familiar bible verses that are typically not fully understood.

Isa 40:31 But they that wait upon the LORD shall renew *their* strength; they shall mount up with wings as eagles; they shall run, and not be weary; *and* they shall walk, and not faint.

This bible verse contains two statements that are seldom taught. First, what does "waiting" on the Lord mean? Well it may mean something to you personally, but it has a very powerful and specific application in scripture.

During the *Great Tribulation* Jerusalem will be overrun with armies. The only way for people to survive is not to run away but to "wait" in Mount Zion in Jerusalem. They are "waiting" for the Messiah to save them from the armies.

Isa 25:9 And it shall be said in that day, Lo, this *is* our God; we have waited for him, and he will save us: this *is* the LORD; we have waited for him, we will be glad and rejoice in his salvation.

Also see Isa 30:18.

The second statement in Isaiah 40:31 is "they shall mount up with wings as eagles". Again, this verse may hold some personal meaning, but the term "eagle's wings" is used in scripture to indicate God's supernatural help given to the Israelites in time of flight. It was applied to Israel's exodus out of Egypt.

Exodus 19:4 Ye have seen what I did unto the Egyptians, and *how* I bare you on eagles' wings, and brought you unto myself.

God carried the Jewish people out of Egypt like an Eagle carries her young. In the next bible verse Moses explains how an eagle caries her young.

Deu 32:11 As an eagle stirreth up her nest, fluttereth over her young, spreadeth abroad her wings, taketh them, beareth them on her wings:

In the future God will bear the Israelis on "eagle's wings" two more times. First, the inhabitants of Judah will flee to the mountains when they see the Antichrist sitting in the holy place (2Th 2:4). God will help the Jews to flee to Jordan. For more bible verses about Judea's flight also see Mark 13:14

Rev 12:14 And to the woman were given two wings of a great eagle, that she might fly into the wilderness, into

her place, where she is nourished for a time, and times, and half a time, from the face of the serpent.

Finally God will give "eagles wings" to the residue of the inhabitants of Jerusalem who didn't run but instead "waited" in Mount Zion at Christ's return at the end of the "Great Tribulation" (Isa 40:31, Zec 14:3-5).

Isa 40:31 But they that wait upon the LORD shall renew *their* strength; they shall mount up with wings as eagles; they shall run, and not be weary; *and* they shall walk, and not faint.

The term "eagle's wings" is used in scripture to indicate God's supernatural help given to the Israelites in time of flight away from their enemies.

SECTION 7: JORDAN

Today about ten percent of Jordan's population consists of refugees from Syria! When Damascus is destroyed many more Syrian refugees will flood into Jordan. They will head for the Jordanian town of Kerak.

Jordan will also be the home of many Israeli refugees during the Great Tribulation. They may also head for Kerak in Moab of Jordan. There is an ancient fortress there. Jordan will eventually turn against these Jewish refugees.

Jordan will also escape the clutches of the Antichrist!

Dan 11:41 He shall enter also into the glorious land, and many *countries* shall be overthrown: but these shall escape out of his hand, *even* Edom, and Moab, and the chief of the children of Ammon.

In the verse above, Edom, Moab, and Ammon are all ancient provinces in the country we now call Jordan.

Chapter Eighteen

Psalm 83 War

Hidden in a secret place!

By Craig C. White

Photo by Ian W. Scott

Judean wilderness east of Jerusalem toward Jordan

Note: The path that sweeps across the illustration is an infamous trail. This may be the route that the people of Judea take while fleeing into the mountains (Mark 13:14).

It is very popular these days to say that the Psalm 83 war will happen soon. Well it will happen pretty soon, but not before the Rapture of the Church, and not before the Great Tribulation. It will happen during the Great Tribulation. Psalm 83 is short and simple. The key to understanding it is to recognize who "*thy hidden ones*" are in verse 3. They are Jews from Judea (region south of Jerusalem) who have fled into the wilderness during the second half of the Great Tribulation. The wilderness is the mountainous region of Jordan east of Jerusalem.

Mark 13:14 But when ye shall see the abomination of desolation, spoken of by Daniel the prophet, standing where it ought not, (let him that readeth understand,) then let them that be in Judaea flee to the mountains:

Psalm 83 is a request for God's help. It probably represents the Judean refugee's call for defense at the end of the Tribulation. Jesus Christ will come through Jordan defeating Israel's enemies (read Revelation Wrath Path). In the verse below, Edom and Bozrah are in today's Jordan.

Isa 63:1 Who *is* this that cometh from Edom, with dyed garments from Bozrah? this *that is* glorious in his apparel, travelling in the greatness of his strength? I that speak in righteousness, mighty to save.

Psalm 83 has four sections; God, be not still, Counsel Council, List of enemies, and Do unto others as you have done unto them before!

God, be not still!

Psalm 83:1 A Song *or* Psalm of Asaph. Keep not thou silence, O God: hold not thy peace, and be not still, O God.

The word *not* is used three times in the opening verse of Psalm 83. The Hebrew word translated *not* here means not!

This is a prayer that God would not allow the people of Israel to be killed by their enemies. Also that God would not fail to devise an offense against Israel's enemies. And that God would not be idle while Israel's enemies attack. In other words, Lord now is the time for action!

Psalm 83:2 For, lo, thine enemies make a tumult: and they that hate thee have lifted up the head.

Israel's enemies hate Israel. The enemies of Israel are the adversaries of God. They are making a loud sound. They are enraged. They are screaming to make war on the Judean refugees. They hate God personally. The word translated *head* in the verse above is the Hebrew word *rosh*. Rosh means chief or primary. It probably refers to a leader. Israel's enemies have magnified their leader. They think that they can fight against God because their ruler is supreme!

Counsel Council

Psalm 83:3 They have taken crafty counsel against thy people, and consulted against thy hidden ones.

God's enemies have assembled together in a secret meeting and have devised a cunning plan against the nation of Israel to utterly destroy them. They have deliberated together to kill God's "*hidden ones*".

In verse 3 above, the term "*hidden ones*" means to hide by covering over. The Judean refugees are protected in mountainous dens in Jordan. They are kept in a secret place until Jesus Christ returns!

In Isaiah 16 below, God allows the Jews escaping Judah to take refuge in Moab which is in today's Jordan east of the Dead Sea. This verse is applied to the time just before Jesus Christ takes his place on his throne in Jerusalem.

Isa 16:3-5 Take counsel, execute judgment; make thy shadow as the night in the midst of the noonday; hide the outcasts; bewray not him that wandereth. 4 Let mine outcasts dwell with thee, Moab; be thou a covert to them from the face of the spoiler: for the extortioner is at an end, the spoiler ceaseth, the oppressors are consumed out of the land. 5 And in mercy shall the throne be established: and he shall sit upon it in truth in the tabernacle of David, judging, and seeking judgment, and hasting righteousness.

In the middle of the Great Tribulation Jews in Judea will flee to the mountains or wilderness. Some of the people of Judea (region around Jerusalem) will *flee to the mountains* where God will sustain them for three and a half years (Mat 24:15-16, Luke 21:21-22). I think that this place is on the east side of the Jordan River near Jericho and Mt. Nebo, where Israel entered the land after the exodus. It is also the place where ravens fed Elijah as he hid (1Ki 17:3). It is also the place where King David and his men fled out of Jerusalem from Absalom his son when he took over the kingdom of Israel (2Sa 17:22).

Mark 13:14 But when ye shall see the abomination of desolation, spoken of by Daniel the prophet, standing where it ought not, (let him that readeth understand,) then let them that be in Judaea flee to the mountains:

Rev 12:6 And the woman fled into the wilderness, where she hath a place prepared of God, that they should feed her there a thousand two hundred *and* threescore days.

Rev 12:14 And to the woman were given two wings of a great eagle, that she might fly into the wilderness, into her place, where she is nourished for a time, and times, and half a time, from the face of the serpent.

Note: In the verse above "Wings of a great eagle" refers to God's supernatural help given to Israel in time of flight. This idiom is applied to Israel during the exodus in Exo 19:4. It is also applied to Israel's deliverance from Jerusalem at the end of the Great Tribulation in Isa 40:31. It is applied here to the people in Judea just before Israel is overrun with its enemies during the Great Tribulation period.

Below; Zechariah tells us that Jesus will save *"the tents of Judah"* before he saves the city of Jerusalem!

Zec 12:7 The LORD also shall save the tents of Judah first, that the glory of the house of David and the glory of the inhabitants of Jerusalem do not magnify *themselves* against Judah.

It may be that *"the tents of Judah"* (above) are those of Judea who fled to the Jordanian mountains. They have been living there for 3 ½ years protected by God.

Base map credit www.cia.gov

Psalm 83 War Map

Psalm 83 is describing a Jordanian conference where Lebanon and Iraq agree to help Jordan eliminate the Jewish refugees who have fled from southern Israel into the mountainous wilderness of western Jordan.

Psalm 83:4 They have said, Come, and let us cut them off from *being* a nation; that the name of Israel may be no more in remembrance. 5 For they have consulted together with one consent: they are confederate against thee:

During their meeting, Israel's enemies plan to destroy the nation of Israel. They have deliberated together and all agree. They have made a pact with themselves. This is describing a Middle Eastern conference were a contract is written that all nations agree to. They will completely eradicate the nation of Israel.

List of enemies

Psalm 83:6 The tabernacles of Edom, and the Ishmaelites; of Moab, and the Hagarenes; 7 Gebal, and Ammon, and Amalek; the Philistines with the inhabitants of Tyre; 8 Assur also is joined with them: they have holpen the children of Lot. Selah.

This list of Israel's enemies is mostly describing the nation of Jordan. Edom is in today's Jordan. Ishmaelites settled Saudi Arabia, but I don't think that Saudi Arabia is represented here. Ishmaelites also settled in today's southern Jordan. Hagarenes settled in today's Jordan, There is a Gebal in Lebanon, but this Gebal is in today's Jordan. Ammon settled in today's Jordan, Amalek probably lived just west of today's Jordan. The Philistines lived on Israel's Mediterranean coast. I think they represent Lebanon here, along with Tyre. Assur is ancient Assyria. Today it is best represented by northern Iraq. So Lebanon and Iraq agree to help the children of Lot. Lot's children were Moab and Ammon. Like I said before, they both settled in today's Jordan.

SECTION 8: IRAN

Will Iran get nuclear weapons? I don't know. Maybe they will. Will they bomb Israel? Not according to the bible. Will they bomb anybody else? There is biblical evidence that Iran and the Kurds will destroy one city during the end time. Revelation 17:5 refers to that city as *Mystery Babylon.* Saudi Arabia is Iran's greatest enemy. I think that the city called Mystery Babylon is in Arabia. My bet is that Iran and the Kurds will destroy the city of Dubai in the United Arab Emirates! Dubai is the closest major Arabian city from Iran's border. It is only 60 miles across the Persian Gulf from Iran's shores!

I think that Iran will also join Iraq and the Kurds in the plundering of the northern Iraq city of Mosul after it is flooded.

Also Iran will join Turkey in an invasion into Israel. I think that this invasion will happen after Turkey destroys Damascus, Syria. Hezbollah militia from Iran is fighting in Syria today.

Chapter Nineteen

Iran in bible prophecy
By Craig C. White

Turkey, Iran, Libya "members of the same family"

The battle of Gog and Magog is brewing! Turkey will lead Libya, Iran, and Sudan in an invasion into Israel! Ezekiel 38 tells us about a Turkish led invasion into Israel. This is called "the battle of Gog and Magog". Gog is Turkey. Magog is its ruler.

Ezekiel 38:5 Persia, Ethiopia, and Libya with them; all of them with shield and helmet:

Today all of these nations are in one accord against Israel. Plus they all have troops fighting inside of Syria. After the destruction of Damascus, all of these armies are likely to turn south into Israel as Ezekiel 38 predicts!

Iranian Foreign Minister Ali Akbar Salehi addressed reports claiming Israel is contemplating an attack on his country, saying: "Iran has always been threatened by Israel. This is nothing new."

In an interview with Turkey's Hurriyet Daily News, Salehi warned that if any country attempts to assault Iran, the Islamic Republic is prepared to retaliate. "We are very certain of our powers. We can defend our country," he claimed.

Commenting on the relationship between Turkey, Syria, and Iran, the Foreign Minister said the three nations are "members of the same family". If one is in trouble, another one will come to its help.

Today Iranians are fighting in Syria against Syrian President Assad. The Turkish Army is amassed on Syria's border. Hezbollah fighters from Sudan are also fighting in Syria.

101

The Turkish led battle of Gog and Magog is the major prophetic event of our time. Today Turkey has a leader that fits the Magog profile. His name is Recep Tayyip Erdogan. He became Prime Minister of Turkey in 2003. He is a devout Muslim and has an ingrained animosity toward Israel. He also has a volatile disposition. He has been over-zealous in his public hatred and provocation toward Israel. While most Middle Eastern despots are being besieged and exiled, Now President Erdogan is popular and gaining in popularity. Erdogan has continued to publicly overstate his condemnation of Israel.

More from High Time to Awake

Available from Amazon.com, CreateSpace.com, and other retail outlets. Also available on Kindle and other devices.

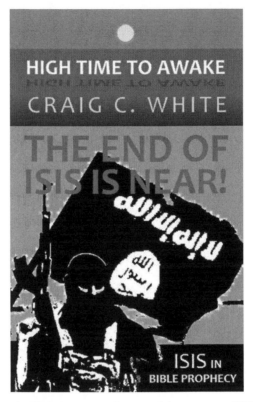

The End of ISIS is near thoroughly covers ISIS in bible prophecy. It also contains a collection of commentaries about present day prophecy whose subjects are current and widely varied.

What is really going on in the world? Will Al-Qaeda take Baghdad? Is all the fighting in the Middle East related? Why is Russia creating a Union? Has Egypt seen the last of the Muslim Brotherhood? What is the Pope up to? Will the Turkey-Israeli reconciliation agreement have a seven year term?

SECTION 9: KURDS

The Kurds are the ancient Medes. Isaiah 21 describes the past destruction of Babylon and also the future destruction of Mystery Babylon. I think Mystery Babylon is Dubai. Just as the Medes and Persians destroyed Babylon in the past, the Kurds and Iran may destroy Mystery Babylon in the future.

The Medes (Kurds) also joined Persia (Iran), and the Babylonians (Iraq) in 612 BC to plunder the city of Nineveh after it was flooded. Nineveh was the capital of the Assyrian Empire. Today the city of Mosul, Iraq is built around the ruins of Nineveh. Mosul is the hometown of Al-Qaeda in Iraq. Al-Qaeda in Iraq is also known as ISIS. The Prophet Nahum tells us that, that "place" will be destroyed with a flood. I think that ISIS in Mosul will again be destroyed by a flood and then be plundered by the Kurds, Iraq, and Iran! You can read all about it in my new book "The End of ISIS is near!"

Chapter Twenty

Mystery Babylon; Party till you Perish

The Feast of Belshazzar
The Writing on the Wall c. 1635 by Rembrandt

A tale of two cities

Isaiah 21:4

By Craig C. White

It is my contention that "MYSTERY BABYLON THE GREAT, THE MOTHER OF HARLOTS AND ABOMINATIONS OF THE EARTH." in Revelation 17:5 is in fact the city of Dubai. You may read my treatise titled "Dubai: a Case for Mystery Babylon". Whichever end time city is Mystery Babylon this commentary watches like a fly on the wall at its last day.

This commentary looks at the very day and very way of the destruction of *that great city* described in Revelation 17:18. Just like ancient Babylon, the modern city called Mystery

Babylon will be in the midst of a drunken party when its destruction comes suddenly!

You are probably familiar with the story of the fall of the ancient city of Babylon (Dan 5:1-6). The once powerful Babylonian empire was on the brink of failing. The king in Babylon was bunkered within the city gates with his princes. The princes were gathered to the city of Babylon because their provinces were already overthrown by the Medes and the Persians. The city was the last stronghold of the Empire. The Medes had besieged the city for months, and were about to break through its walls. Belshazzar, king in Babylon was yet prideful. He thought that nobody would conquer the walled city. In an effort to demonstrate his self-confident supremacy he decided to host a party. At that time the people of Israel (that is Judah) were captives in Babylon. Belshazzar further demonstrated his preeminence by drinking from the holy vessels taken from the Jerusalem temple. During the drunken party Belshazzar noticed a disembodied hand over by the punch bowl, writing a salutation on the wall.

MENE, MENE, TEKEL, UPHARSIN (Dan 5:25).

God hath numbered thy kingdom, and finished it. Thou art weighed in the balances, and art found wanting. Thy kingdom is divided, and given to the Medes and Persians (Dan 5:26-28).

That very night Belshazzar was killed and the Mede and Persian Empire conquered the Babylonian Empire (Dan 5:30-31). In much the same way Mystery Babylon will fall in the future.

There is a principle in bible prophecy; that some prophecies have two distinct applications. They apply to two separate events usually separated by time. This is the case with several prophecies regarding the demise of ancient Babylon. They also apply to MYSTERY BABYLON. Mystery Babylon is a city that exists during the Great

Tribulation. We are going to look at a section of scripture in Isaiah that pertains to the fall of ancient Babylon, and then we will look at a section in Jeremiah. Let's start by looking at Isaiah.

Isa 13:6-11 Howl ye; for the day of the LORD is at hand; it shall come as a destruction from the Almighty. 7 Therefore shall all hands be faint, and every man's heart shall melt: 8 And they shall be afraid: pangs and sorrows shall take hold of them; they shall be in pain as a woman that travaileth: they shall be amazed one at another; their faces shall be as flames. 9 Behold, the day of the LORD cometh, cruel both with wrath and fierce anger, to lay the land desolate: and he shall destroy the sinners thereof out of it. 10 For the stars of heaven and the constellations thereof shall not give their light: the sun shall be darkened in his going forth, and the moon shall not cause her light to shine. 11 And I will punish the world for their evil, and the wicked for their iniquity; and I will cause the arrogancy of the proud to cease, and will lay low the haughtiness of the terrible.

Remember that these verses pertain to the judgment of Babylon. The above verses describe *the day of the LORD* (Joel 2:31). *The day of the LORD* occurs during, and at the end of the Great Tribulation period in the future. So evidently this verse also applies to future events.

Isa 13:17 Behold, I will stir up the Medes against them, which shall not regard silver; and as for gold, they shall not delight in it.

As we saw earlier, the Medes did overthrow the city of ancient Babylon. It occurs to me that they might also overthrow Mystery Babylon in the future.

Isa 21:1 The burden of the desert of the sea. As whirlwinds in the south pass through; so it cometh from the desert, from a terrible land.

The verse above applies much better to Dubai than it does to Babylon in Iraq. The original city of Babylon is nowhere near a sea. Dubai is on the Persian Gulf in the Saudi desert. Also notice that the whirlwinds come from the desert in the south. That is true for Dubai. In Iraq the desert is on the west.

Isa 21:2 A grievous vision is declared unto me; the treacherous dealer dealeth treacherously, and the spoiler spoileth. Go up, O Elam: besiege, O Media; all the sighing thereof have I made to cease.

Elam is ancient Persia or modern Iran. Media refers to the Medes or roughly the area of Northern Iraq, and Eastern Turkey. Today the Kurds represent the ancient Medes. Just as they destroyed Babylon in the past, they may destroy Dubai in the future.

Isa 21:3 Therefore are my loins filled with pain: pangs have taken hold upon me, as the pangs of a woman that travaileth: I was bowed down at the hearing of it; I was dismayed at the seeing of it.

This describes Belshazzar's reaction to the writing on the wall. This same language is used to describe the fear of the nations in *the day of the LORD* (1Th 5:3, Jer 49:22).

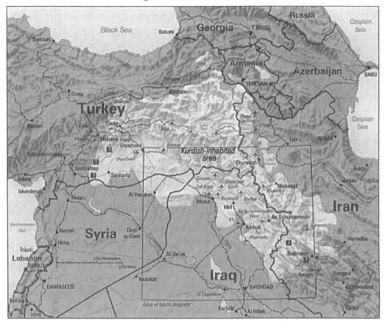

Map credit: www.cia.gov

Modern Kurdish inhabited area

The Kurds live in northern Iraq, eastern Syria, and eastern Turkey. They have separate status from the rest of Iraq. The Kurds have their own government and military. The Kurds are the ancient Medes. Isaiah 21:2 above describes the past destruction of Babylon and also the future destruction of Mystery Babylon. I think Mystery Babylon is Dubai. The Kurds and the Iranians will destroy Dubai!

Isa 21:4 My heart panted, fearfulness affrighted me: the night of my pleasure hath he turned into fear unto me. 5 Prepare the table, watch in the watchtower, eat, drink: arise, ye princes, and anoint the shield.

Above describes the banqueting of the princes of Babylon. Their party was interrupted by an invasion. I suspect that like ancient Babylon, Dubai may be in the midst of a drunken party at the moment of their sudden demise.

Isa 21:9 And, behold, here cometh a chariot of men, with a couple of horsemen. And he answered and said, Babylon is fallen, is fallen; and all the graven images of her gods he hath broken unto the ground.

This same language that describes the fall of Babylon here also describes the fall of "Mystery Babylon" in Revelation 14:8.

Rev 14:8 And there followed another angel, saying, Babylon is fallen, is fallen, that great city, because she made all nations drink of the wine of the wrath of her fornication.

Now let's look at Jeremiah.

Jer 51:6 Flee out of the midst of Babylon, and deliver every man his soul: be not cut off in her iniquity; for this is the time of the LORD'S vengeance; he will render unto her a recompence.

People are warned to come out of ancient Babylon above. They are also warned to come out of Mystery Babylon during the Great Tribulation in Revelation below.

Rev 18:4 And I heard another voice from heaven, saying, Come out of her, my people, that ye be not partakers of her sins, and that ye receive not of her plagues.

Jer 51:7 Babylon hath been a golden cup in the LORD'S hand, that made all the earth drunken: the nations have drunken of her wine; therefore the nations are mad.

Belshazzar's party guests drank from the holy vessels taken from the temple in Jerusalem. Likewise God has used Babylon and its philosophy of idolatry and world conquest to pollute the nations since. Any party that is pressing toward "the New World Order" or "One World Government" is drunk with Babylonian wine.

Jer 51:8-9 Babylon is suddenly fallen and destroyed: howl for her; take balm for her pain, if so be she may be healed. 9 We would have healed Babylon, but she is not healed: forsake her, and let us go every one into his own country: for her judgment reacheth unto heaven, and is lifted up even to the skies.

Babylon is best known for its high tower. It represented world unity without obligation to God. This is the kingdom that Satan longs for. Today, Dubai stands for the same thing. They have built their tower to heaven. Their judgment will match.

Jer 51:13 O thou that dwellest upon many waters, abundant in treasures, thine end is come, and the measure of thy covetousness.

In bible prophecy "many waters" often pertains to "many nations". This can describe the nations of the world today that are imbibed with Babylonian ideals. It is also appropriate to describe Dubai's situation as it is built on the Arabian Sea with many manmade islands. One could easily describe Dubai as *abundant in treasures*.

Jer 51:27-28 Set ye up a standard in the land, blow the trumpet among the nations, prepare the nations against her, call together against her the kingdoms of Ararat, Minni, and Ashchenaz; appoint a captain against her; cause the horses to come up as the rough caterpillers. 28 Prepare against her the nations with the kings of the Medes, the captains thereof, and all the rulers thereof, and all the land of his dominion.

The kingdoms listed here, "Ararat, Minni, and Ashchenaz" are part of ancient Media. Today they are the nation of Armenia. Notice in verse 28 that "all the land of his dominion" is prepared for war against Babylon. All of ancient Media was prepared for war against Babylon under the leadership of Darius. The text seems to emphasize Armenia; however, in the future battle against Mystery

111

Babylon, Along with Iran and Iraq; Armenia may be joined with Georgia, and Azerbaijan, the territories of ancient Media. In my commentary titled "The Leopard is Upon Us" I explain how these countries may soon come under the control of Russia. In verse 27 a captain is appointed over the armies. Caterpillars are locust, or cankerworms. They describe a large devouring army. This similitude is used in several prophetic bible passages.

Jer 51:53 Though Babylon should mount up to heaven, and though she should fortify the height of her strength, yet from me shall spoilers come unto her, saith the LORD.

As it was in Babylon it will be in Mystery Babylon. The Dubai Tower (Burj Khalifa) is the tallest in the world at 2,684 feet.

Jer 51:57 And I will make drunk her princes, and her wise men, her captains, and her rulers, and her mighty men: and they shall sleep a perpetual sleep, and not wake, saith the King, whose name is the LORD of hosts.

The princes of Babylon got drunk out of the holy vessels. God will give them their desires. They will drink and never awake from their stupor. As it was in Babylon it will be in Mystery Babylon.

BONUS SECTION: BURMA?

Chapter Twenty One

Burma in Bible Prophecy

Spot the leopard's wing

By Craig C. White

U.S. President Barack Obama is traveling to Burma to attend a South Eastern Asian summit. The priority given to Burma at this time may have biblical prophetic implication. There is an effort underway to create a United Central Asian Confederacy. The main countries involved are Turkmenistan, Afghanistan, Pakistan, and India. Other adjacent countries will also participate. Daniel chapter 7 explains the formation of the final gentile world empire, or as we call it today "The New World Order". In Daniel 7:6 the formation of a United Central Asian Union is described. As in all bible prophecy a beast represents a gentile kingdom. This beast is represented by a leopard and has *four heads* (or main nations), and *four wings* (or secondary nations). Burma is in the region and may be one of the four secondary nations that form the new United Central Asian Union. I think that the formation of the United Central Asian Confederacy will now be a major priority for U.S. President Barack Obama and other world leaders. We will probably hear a lot more about it soon. We should all be on the lookout for this Central Asian Union represented by the Leopard. It is High Time to Awake!

###

By the way, if you review this book on Amazon I will let you park in the pastors parking space next Sunday!

Thank you in advance, Craig C. White

About the Author

Craig C. White

Craig C. White was born in 1958 and born again in 1964. In the 1980's he was an active member of Calvary Church in Santa Ana, California. The expositional bible teaching of then pastor Dr. David Hocking played a major role in building Craig's biblical literacy. He has been a serious bible student ever since.

The views contained in my commentaries are solely my own. I do not accept other views just because they are popular. I try to understand what the bible says. You will find clear interpretations here that you will scarcely find elsewhere.

Made in the USA
Middletown, DE
03 October 2016